'UNDERSTANDING ISMAILISM' examines the substance and practice of Ismailism with a penetrating study considering these fundamental aspects:

- Inner mystiques of Ismaili Tariqah (Ismailism)
- Esoteric values of Ismaili beliefs
- Equivocal 'Declaration of Faith'
- Enigmatic perception of Prophethood vis a vis Imamat
- Unfettered power and authority of an Imam – the Spiritual Father and Mother of Ismailis
- Inexplicable translations of 'reconstituted' Quranic verses
- Unique teachings of the Assassins and its aftermath
- Perplexing legends transcending into "historical facts"
- Fascinating history of Ismaili Imams, corroborated and contradicted by Ismaili authors
- Also, many many unforgettable anecdotes

PLUS

- An analytical study and a comprehensive comparison of Judaism, Christianity and Islam.

ISBN 0-9693571-0-9

$7.00

A.M. TRUST • P.O. BOX 82584 • BURNABY, B.C. • CANADA V5C 5Z1

UNDERSTANDING
ISMAILISM

A Unique
Tariqah of Islam

by

AKBARALLY MEHERALLY

Library of Congress Cataloging in Publication Data

Meherally, Akbarally
Understanding Ismailism

ISBN 0-9693571-0-9

A.M. Trust
P.O. Box 82584
BURNABY, B.C.
Canada V5C 5Z1

Typeset by G.T. Laser's Edge Ltd.
Printed in Canada – 1988
Printed by Northburn Printers

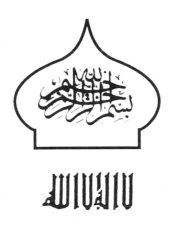

Bismillahir Rehmanir Raheem
In The Name of Allah
The All-Merciful, The All-Compassionate
There is no god but the God.

All praise be to Allah - *Subhanahu wa ta'ala,*
Glorified and Exalted.

May Allah grant me the *Taufiq,*
to speak the truth and spread His words.

Al-Quran

– the Sacred Book for mankind.

This Heavenly Book has been my *'Furqan'* – the Criterion, a standard of judgement.

It has showed me the right path as my Guide *(Imam)* and Light *(Noor)*, the same way it guided, 1400 years ago, the pagan Arabs to distinguish and discriminate between good and evil, to rid them of their agelong superstitions, idolatory and various customs of the "age of ignorance".

I have quoted verses from this final scripture – the Quran, with intent and prayers that these few, out of over 6200 verses, may be a Guide and a Warner to the readers.

"Say: Lo! my Lord hurleth the Truth.
(He is) the knower of things hidden."
Holy Quran 34/48

Contents

1

Introduction

Faith blooms with understanding. The expansion of understanding makes for an expansion of trust, and reading widens the horizons of understanding. If one was to step into a public library and scan a computer listing, or go through a catalog under the heading Islam, he would discover enough titles to expand his understanding of Islamic history and Islam. But, if he was to search under the heading Ismailism or Ismailis, he would hardly come across a book written by an Ismaili author or published by an Ismaili institution that would open a door and invite him to examine the *Tariqah* (practices) or the history of Ismailism, from inside out.

Recently, I came across two publications written in English, by Al-Waiz Abualy A. Aziz. Both of these books — *Ismaili Tariqah* and *A Brief History of Ismailism* — were published in Canada in 1985.

Al-Waiz Abualy is the senior most *Al-Waiz* (Missionary) who has devoted his entire life propagating the Ismaili Tariqah (Ismailism) for and on behalf of the Aga Khan's international institution for the propagation of faith and publication of religious literatures. This institution is called "The Shia Imami Ismaili Tariqah and Religious Education Board." Al-Waiz Abualy is also the author of over a dozen books on the subjects of Ismaili faith and its history. His favourite subjects are the esoteric aspects of Ismaili beliefs and the history of Ismaili *Imams* (Leaders) and Ismaili *Pirs* (Teachers - *Dais*).

I have known Abualy since the early forties when I joined the "Recreation Club" in Bombay, India as a student missionary. Later the "Club" changed its name to "Ismailia Association", and under the new Constitution promulgated recently by Karim Aga Khan, the Association is now known as "The Shia Imami Ismaili Tariqah and Religious Education Board". In effect, the so called "Club" has come out of its disguise. During the days when I joined the Recreation Club as a mission student, Abualy was one of the youngest teachers to our group. I did not end up as a missionary propagating the Ismaili doctrines but I continued my research and studies.

Treat my Jamat psychologically

During the last forty years of my close association with the Ismaili community as an active member of the *Jamat* (Community), I have studied the principles, practices and teachings of the Ismaili Tariqah from close quarters. As a past President of an Ismailia Council I had the opportunity to observe the norms of leadership as well as conduction of Leadership Conventions and Conferences at all levels. One piece of advice that I received personally from the top authority was to **treat my Jamat psychologically.** I have watched Jamati leaders do exactly this. When the request was for desperately needed financial assistance, the Jamat was treated with the psychology developed by the famous Viennese physician Sigmund Freud. I have observed Ismaili preachers who would feed the congregation with pep talks for days, when what was required were actual facts on the fundamental and basic issues. This practice has been so common that a lot of the younger generation and middle aged adults walk out of the *Jamalkhanas* (prayer houses), before the preachers reach the pulpits.

Experienced missionaries who have been in the business of preaching and teaching for a long time have learned that the audience that remains behind to hear the sermon is composed mainly of *Bhagats* (genuine devotees), who are used to hearing pep talks and not the Truth. They have to keep on harping the same tune that the Ismaili Pirs have recited in their devotional songs *(Ginans)*. The moment they step outside of this well trodden path they will be disqualified by the Jamat and reprimanded by the Board. I can never forget one such typical example that I had the misfortune of witnessing in one of the Jamatkhanas in Burnaby, Canada.

Human Compositions and Divine Revelations

A husband and wife team of young missionaries was officially invited by the Ismailia Association from The Islamic Republic of Pakistan to give a series of lectures on Islam and Ismailism. The subject for that night's sermon, suggested by the Ismailia Association was **Comparison of the Ginanic verses with the Quranic verses**. Ginans are very near and dear to Ismailis because they were composed by Ismaili Pirs who had converted their forefathers. Ismailis recite these Ginans each and every day in their Jamatkhanas throughout the world. Professionally recorded Ginans are sold for home listening.

The husband of the team began his lecture by pointing out an Islamic point of view. The word "comparison" in the title of his sermon was inappropriate. The Quran is a Divine Revelation revealed by Allah Himself whereas Ginans were composed by men and women. No Muslim can ever think of comparing a human composition with the most Sublime, Unparalleled Supreme composition. What he said was Pure Truth. It is said that only a lion's cub can digest the milk of a lioness. A large section of the congregation, male and female, walked out in silent protest. The young missionary coming from an Islamic State could not believe his eyes nor could he control his frustration and anger. He discontinued his sermon and left the pulpit. After much persuasion from the Executive Officers of the Jamat and the Association, the team resumed their lecture. They made a request that those who did not hold similar views should leave and let others hear the rest of their sermon. Practically half the Jamat left the Jamatkhana. Some were not interested in the teachings of the Quran. Others could not bear to hear the undisputed facts about the Ginans.

This attitude stands true also for the published literature. The majority of these people have never even opened the Book of Islamic scripture - the Quran — even though they call themselves Muslims. Ismailis would not touch any literature that disagrees with the Ginanic teachings of their Pirs and *Farmans* (Commands) of their Imams. One of the Farmans of Aga Khan III made during his first trip of Zanzibar, Africa tells Ismailis not to read books other than that written by Pir Sadruddin, which are known as Ginans.

I have spent most of my life as a devout Ismaili having studied as well as practiced, both the esoteric and exoteric form of Ismaili Tariqah; paying 12 1/2 % of my **gross** income before taxes and expenses, as Dasond *(Zakat)* in Jamatkhana. In 1976, I went for the change of 'key-word' for meditation called *Isme-Azam* (great name). After 30 years of esoteric *Zikr-Ibadah* (meditation), I was given a *Naksh* (key-calligraphy) and told this was the highest stage of *Baitul Khayal Bandgi*. I was asked not to come back for any higher grade or classes because there is none higher.

Are you not afraid?

Today, as a devout Muslim, I look back at all that I have been taught, practiced and propagated. In Canada I have had the opportunity of reading books of all religions. I came across articles and papers on Ismailism and Islam written by various authors. I compared what I had learned and what I was learning. I tried to understand Ismailism. In the process I started asking questions to individuals, missionaries, local Ismaili leaders, top ranking international leaders and even to the Imam by direct letters, as well as by memorandums through official channels, as prescribed in the Constitution . . . I got no response.

One day, an international head of the Ismailia Association came to see me at my place of business. He happens to be a friend of mine for a couple of decades. He asked me a question: "Akbar Bhai, are you not afraid that *Mawla Bapa* (Aga Khan) may get displeased with you?". I replied, "Why should I be afraid, all I'm doing is asking questions to understand the religion? Is not Mawla Bapa a Guide (*an Imam*)?"

"How should I fear that which ye set up beside Him, when ye fear not to set up beside Allah that for which He hath revealed

– 5 –

unto you no warrant? Which of the two fac-
tions hath more right to safety? (answer me
that) if ye have knowledge".

Holy Quran 6/82

(The translation, including the words within
the brackets, is by M.M. Pickthall. In Yusuf
Ali's translation the verse number is 81.)

2

Unique Tariqah

In the book 'Ismaili Tariqah', Al-Waiz Abualy A. Aziz — one of the senior missionaries of the Ismaili faith — writes on Page 132:

"Ismaili Tariqah is unique. It has a direct link with Ali and Nabi"

The Ismaili sect is a minority sect of the Shia Tariqah of Islam. Nearly one million followers of Aga Khan call themselves "The Shia Imami Ismaili Muslims." The reported figure of 15 million followers of Aga Khan is a gross exaggeration based upon conjecture. The Islamic *Ummah* (Universal Brotherhood of Muslims) is a fraternity of nearly one billion Muslims. Sunni Muslims, the majority group in Islam, comprise 90% of the Ummah.

Shiatu-Ali (Party of Ali), popularly known as the Shia Muslims, is the minority group in Islam. It comprises only 9% of the Muslim brotherhood.

The only Tariqah acceptable by Allah!

The fact that the Ismaili Tariqah is the only Tariqah that will be acceptable to Allah on the Day of Judgment; all other sects of Islam be rejected by Allah, is a popular belief and a deep rooted impression upon Ismaili minds. To substantiate their claim, Ismailis often quote a *Hadith*, the reported saying of Prophet (peace and blessings of Allah be upon him) which says that after the Prophet Muhammad's passing away, Islam will be divided into 73 sects. Of these 73 sects, only one will be on the right path and acceptable on the day of Judgment and the rest will be rejected or worthy of damnation. The obvious question is why is it the Ismaili Tariqah, followed by 1 million out of 1,000 million Muslims, will be the only one acceptable from the 73 Tariqahs?

According to Ismaili teachings and preachings, the Ismaili Tariqah is at the top most level of the esoteric vision called *Batiniyat* or *Marifat*. The rest of the Islamic Tariqahs are on the levels of either *Shariyat*, *Tariqat*, or *Haqiqat*. For example, a Muslim who is on the level of 'Shariyat' would perform an ablution (*Wadu*) of his physical body before reciting his *Salat* or *Namaz* (Ritual Prayers). Whereas, an Ismaili who believes himself to be a *Marfati Momin,* possesses an esoteric vision and knowledge which guides him to comprehend that it is the Spiritual Soul that needs the cleansing, and not the Physical Body. Hence, an Ismaili **does not** perform ablution of his physical body like the rest of the Muslims, before reciting his *Dua* (Ritual Prayers for Ismailis). Ismailis call themselves *Batini* and qualify themselves as *Momins*. The logic and the argument that is applied with regard to the performance of physical ablution versus spiritual ablution is also applied by Ismailis to physical fasting (*Saum*), Pilgrimage (*Hajj*), etc.

Abualy writes on page 54 of 'Ismaili Tariqah'

> "They (Ismailis) attach more importance to the object than to the subject of a matter. Spiritual matters are given preference over material things, yet wordly duties and progress are not neglected".

Ismaili Tariqah is not only an esoteric Tariqah, but it is also a *Noorani Tariqah*. Ismailis look upon the 'Noor (Light) of Allah' as having been manifested upon this earth in the body of an *Imam* (Spiritual Leader). For example, a Muslim is one who submits himself entirely to the Will of Allah; an Ismaili 'Momin' is one who submits himself entirely to the Will of Karim Aga Khan who possesses the 'Noor of Allah' within his physical body. When an Ismaili prostrates before his *Hazar* (present) Imam, he prostrates to the 'Noor of Allah' and not to the physical body of the Aga Khan. The same logic and argument holds good for him when he prostrates before the photograph of the Aga Khan in his Jamatkhana while reciting his Dua, seeking forgiveness for his sins or when soliciting help and mercy.

However, there is one fundamental exception to the overall concept of the pre-eminence of the spiritual over the physical in this philosophy: Karim Aga Khan's claim for being the 49th bearer and possessor of the 'Noor of Allah' has to be based upon his being a hereditary **physical lineal descendant** of Hazrat Ali (r.a.), the son-in-law and cousin of the Holy Prophet (s.a.s.). Succession to the Imamat in future will be from amongst his **physical male descendants** only. There can be no exception to this rule, according to the Ismaili Constitution. (updated, and inaugurated in December 1986).

Going back to the original topic of this chapter, viz:

"Ismaili Tariqah is unique. It has a direct link with Ali and Nabi."

We have examined the kind of link Ismaili Momins have developed with Hazrat Ali ibn Abu Talib and his successor, the Aga Khan, but we have yet to examine the link that Ismailis have developed with Nabi, Prophet Muhammad.

Imamat over Naboowat

I quote a paragraph from page 119 of Ismaili Tariqah:

> "Many biographers of the Holy Prophet have reported that the Prophet had the mark of the Seal of Prophethood on his back near the right shoulder. It was a mole, as big as a half an egg of a pigeon. When the Holy Imam stepped on the shoulders of the Holy Prophet, the Seal was under his foot. Lovers of Ali have interpreted this event as a sign of the importance of Imamat over Naboowwat".

Note: This unique quotation needs no comment.

According to Ismaili belief, *Panjtan Pak* (i.e. Hazrat Ali, Prophet Muhammad, Bibi Fatima, Hassan and Hussein) had in them the 'Noor of Allah'. This would mean that Nabi Muhammad **also** possessed the 'Noor of Allah', *but*... But, what? An Ismaili would say that it was not of the same *power* as Ali's. **Nabi – the Prophet, did not have the same authority as Ali, the Imam.** Does that mean the 'Noor of Allah' has different grades? Al-Waiz Abualy, the author of 'Ismaili Tariqah', explains this in more specific terms, on page 129 of his book:

> **"Nabi came to show the Truth**
> **Ali is the possessor of the Truth".**
>
> **"Nabi is the Receiver of the Quran,**
> **Ali the speaking Quran".**

In other words,

a) Imam's *Farmans* (Commands) are The Truth.
b) Imam's word is the Quran.

On a close study of Ismaili rites, rituals and religious practices, one can easily say that Quranic laws have been overshadowed, and in some cases set aside, by the *Farmans* of Imams. We shall observe this in the later chapters.

Unfettered power and authority

On the 13th day of December, 1986 a revised Constitution for The Shia Imami Ismaili Muslims was ordained under the Sign Manual and Seal of Mawlana Hazar Imam Shah Karim al Hussaini, His Highness Prince Aga Khan the 49th Imam of the Shia Imami Ismaili Muslims, at Merimont, Geneva, Switzerland. The very first article of the said Constitution is the 'Power and Authority of Mawlana Hazar Imam'. The first clause of the said article reads:

> 1.1 Mawlana Hazar Imam has inherent right and absolute and ***unfettered power and authority*** over and in respect of ***all religious*** and Jamati matters of the Ismailis.

An Ismaili Momin who has taken an oath of allegiance *(Baiyat)* to his or her Hazar Imam has committed himself or herself to abide by this Constitution and obey the Aga Khan's authority as the **Supreme Authority** over and in respect of **all** religious and Jamati matters.

A Muslim who has not joined this Unique 73rd Tariqah and has not committed himself or herself to this Unique Bondage, submits himself or herself to the one and only **Supreme Constitution**, revealed through their beloved Nabi, Prophet Muhammad, by Allah Himself, the Creator and Sustainer of the Worlds. This Constitution is the Holy Quran and it says:

> "Say: For me, I have an obvious sign from my Lord, but ye reject it. What ye would see hastened is not in my power. *The Command* (authority to command) *rests with none but Allah*: He declares the Truth, and He is the best of Judges."
>
> *Holy Quran 6/57*

3

Unique Fabrication

Most Ismailis have not read the Quran. To this day, they have not paid the respect due to the Revelations of Allah. Nor have they realized the significance and importance of this Divine Message. Hence, the seriousness of fabricating Quranic verses, and its consequences, may not be fully comprehended by an Ismaili Momin. The enormity is far more serious when the intention behind the fabrication is deliberate and is to propagate falsehood, in the name of Allah.

Imam is immaculate and sinless

Al-Waiz Abualy has studied the Quran and has also written a chapter on The Holy Quran in his book 'Ismaili Tariqah'. He has quoted the Quranic verse 33/33, in fragment, on page 124 of this book. The fragmentation is done with a purpose. The fragmented translation reads:

"He (Imam) is the Noor of Allah, therefore, he is immaculate and sinless."

Reproduced below is the complete text of verses 32 and 33 of chapter 33:

"O ye wives of the Prophet! Ye are not like any other women. If ye keep your duty (to Allah), then be not soft of speech, lest he in whose heart is a disease aspire (to you) but utter customary speech. And stay in your houses. Bedizen not yourselves with the bedizenment of the time of ignorance. Be regular in prayer, and pay the poor-due, and obey Allah and His Messenger. Allah's wish is but to remove uncleanness far from you, O folk of the household, and cleanse you with a thorough cleansing."

The verse 33/33 is addressed to **"O ye wives of the prophet"** or to **"O folk of the household"**. It is neither addressed to, nor revealed with respect to, **"He"** or **"Imam"**. In the entire Arabic text of these two verses there is no mention of **"Noor of Allah"**. In the entire Quran there is no mention of **"He (Imam) is Noor of Allah"** or **Ali is Noor of Allah** or **Ali is sinless.**

On the other hand "Book of Law, revealed to Moses", "Gospel sent to Jesus – the son of Mary" and "The Scripture in Truth, revealed upon Muhammad", are designated as **"Noor"** and **"guidance"**. See chapter 5 verses 47 to 51 (in Yusuf Ali's translation) and verses 44 to 48 (in Pickthall's translation).

As for being **"immaculate and sinless"**, the Prophet never ever claimed to be so during his lifetime. How then can a member of the household or a relative of the Prophet claim to be immaculate and sinless by virtue of being a near or distant relative of the Prophet? History shows that Prophet Muhammad and Hazrat Ali both sought forgiveness of their sins from Allah, five times a day or more, until the last days and hours of their existences upon this earth.

Manifestation of 'Noor of Allah' in a human body which is immaculate and sinless – Fact, Fallacy, Fiction or deliberate Fabrication?

As for those who Fabricate, Allah says:

> "Therefore woe be unto those who write the Scripture with their hands and then say, 'This is from Allah', that they may purchase a small gain therewith! Woe unto them for that their hands have written, and woe unto them for that they earn thereby."
>
> *Holy Quran 2/79*

4

Unique
Prevarication

Ali is the Wise

On page 128 of 'Ismaili Tariqah' appears an English translation of the Quranic verse 4 of chapter 43. I have gone through various English, Urdu and Gujarati translations of the Quran and I have yet to find a single translation that would come close to the one the author has published in his book. His *Unique Translation* reads:

"Indeed, to Us, Ali is the Wise as stated in the Mother-book"

Below is the translation of the same verse done by Abdullah Yusuf Ali:

"And Verily, it is in the Mother of the Book, in Our presence, high (in dignity), full of wisdom."

Going through the Arabic text, it appears that the author Abualy has translated the words "Aliyyun Hakiim" as "ALI IS THE WISE".

In the language of the Quran (Arabic):

Al-'Aliyyu means The Exalted or Most High.
Al-Azizu means The Mighty or Supreme.
Al-'Aziimu means The Grand or Tremendous.

These are adjectives, as well as the attributes of Allah. At the same time, Ali, Aziz and Azim are proper names for individuals. The author has substituted one adjective with a proper name and manipulated the entire translation. If his translation mode was to be applied to the Quran, then the entire Quran would read differently, e.g. *Azizun Hakim* would read "Mr. Aziz is Wise". In the celebrated 'Verse of the throne' – *Ayat-ul-Kursi* i.e. chapter 2 verse 255 – the last line which reads "He *(Allah)* is the Exalted, the Grand" could be translated by a dishonest or unscrupulous translator in the following different ways:

a) "Exalted Azim is He *(Allah)*"
b) "Grand Ali is He *(Allah)*".
c) "Ali, Azim (both) are He *(Allah)*".

Similarly, the popular Takbeer **"Allah-O-Akbar"** meaning "Allah is Great" could be deceitfully and dishonourably translated by a Prevaricating Translator as:

"Allah is Akbar" or **"Akbar is Allah"** (May Allah forgive us for reading these blasphemies).

Allah has given every individual the wisdom to distinguish the truth from falsehood. A missionary's duty is to propagate what he is expected or asked by his superiors or masters to propagate.

A reader's duty is to verify the facts with original sources or roots, and then decide what to believe and what not to believe. There is always among us a section who would distort the Scripture and Allah says:

> "There is among them a section who distort the Book with their tongues: (as they read) you would think it is a part of the Book, but it is no part of the Book; and they say, 'That is from Allah. But it is not from Allah: It is they who tell a lie against Allah, and (well) they know it!"
>
> *Holy Quran 3/78*

5

Unique Appointment

"A Brief History of Ismailism" is written and published by Al-Waiz Abualy A. Aziz. It is a "highly recommended" High School text book. This recommendation has been made by the Aga Khan's officially recognized and constitutionally authorized institution for religious education and propagation of Ismaili faith, viz., 'The Shia Imami Ismaili Tariqah and Religious Education Board' (formerly, "Ismailia Association").

Did Allah appoint Ali?

On page 107 of the said book, Missionary Abualy teaches and propagates the following:

"The Imam is the Supreme Authority **appointed directly by Allah**."

The question is, did Allah appoint any individual as **"The Supreme Authority?"** If so, how, when and where? The response that one can find to these questions appears in Abualy's other book, 'Ismaili Tariqah'.

Under the heading **Proclamation of Imamat**, the author writes on page 120:

> "It was Sunday the 18th Zil-Hijja (15th of March, 632). The Holy Prophet delivered a long sermon and at the end informed them (the people who had returned from the pilgrimage) that this was perhaps his last hajj. He declared: "I am leaving behind me the two most important things for you: The Book of Allah and my Ahl-Bait (Progeny). The two will never depart from each other. If you will follow them you will never go astray". He then called Ali near him and **introduced him** to the people, saying: "For those who consider me as their *Mowla* (Master), Ali **too** is their Mowla".

Although the "introduction" designates Ali as **Mowla**, the Ismailis claim it was not a simple "introduction" but a very important **Proclamation** made by the Prophet and that Ali was declared **Imam** (Guide or Leader).

If it is to be professed that **"Mowla" is equal to "Imam"**, then these two points must be considered in consequence:

a) Taking the wording of the "Proclamation" as claimed, one has to admit that the Prophet was already "Mowla" (i.e. Imam) when he proclaimed

Ali **too** as "Mowla" (i.e. Imam). Hence, Prophet Mohammad would be the First Imam and Hazrat Ali the Second Imam. Also, both were "Imams" simultaneously. **To say that Ali was "Imam" and Muhammad was not, would be incorrect.**

b) If what the author claims to have transpired after the final Hajj, did in reality happen (which the majority of Muslims refuse to accept), then the said Proclamation or Appointment of Imamat was **done by the Prophet of Allah** and not **"directly by Allah"**.

To justify his claim, the author adds at the end of the paragraph the following:

> "Finally he (Prophet) told the congregation:
> 'I have delivered you the *message that Allah had commanded* me to do so."

This not unnaturally leads one to enquire:

If the "introduction" or the "Proclamation", which was made before the returning pilgrims, was a **Command** or a **Message** from Allah, then the text of that Command would have been revealed to the Prophet as a *Wahi*, meaning a "Revelation" from Allah. By virtue of being a 'Revelation', the text becomes a part of the 'Book of Revelations' – the Quran. How come this Proclamation/Command has not been included in the Quran when all Messages and Commands, major as well as minor, are included?

As shown in the previous chapters, distortion of the Quranic Message has been a common practice. It has been so frequent and yet uncontested because in the past, the majority of Ismailis had not taken the trouble to read the Quran. Today, more and more Ismailis have started reading the Quran, especially after learning of the distortions being propagated and preached as Ismailism. Here is one more instance of the misrepresentation being propagated by those entrusted with the duty of faithfully spreading knowledge of Ismailism, Islam and Islamic scriptures to the Jamat:

Under the same heading – "Proclamation of Imamat" – the author writes on Page 120 of 'Ismaili Tariqah': "Holy Prophet was returning from his (final) Hajj ceremonies; there were about 120,000 pilgrims with him. When he arrived at a road junction known as Ghadir-e-Khom he received the following Revelation:

> 'O Messenger! Make known that which hath been revealed unto thee from thy Lord, for if thou do it not, thou will not have conveyed His message. Allah will protect thee from mankind. Lo! Allah guideth not the disbelieving folk".

One will find that the above quoted verse appears in Chapter 5 and verse number 67 in Pickthall's translation or verse number 70 in Yusuf Ali's translation. If one is to read the two verses preceding and one verse following the above quoted Revelation, one will see that the above Revelation was revealed to the Prophet in connection with a "Message" that was to be delivered to the *"People of the Books"* i.e. the Jews and the Christians. Even the text of the "Message" to be delivered appears in the next verse. The text begins with:

"Say: O People of the Books!
Ye have ...."

It is an undisputed fact that Jews and Christians were not the fellow travellers of the Prophet Muhammad on his return from the final Hajj. That makes it obvious that the said Revelation was *not* revealed at Ghadir-e-Khom *nor* was it revealed in connection with the Proclamation of the "Imamat" or Introduction of "The Supreme Authority." Now comes the important question – What is the historical version in connection with the affair of Ghadir-e-Khom? The New Encyclopaedia of Islam, Volume II, gives a detailed account of the episode as well as the historical version. The author and compiler of the Encyclopaedia is L. Veccia Vaglieri. He has no axe to grind. He writes:

> "On this point, Ibn Kathir shows himself yet again to be a percipient historian: he connects the affair of Ghadir Khumm with episodes which took place during the expedition to the Yemen, which was led by Ali in 10/631-2, and which had returned to Mecca just in time to meet the Prophet there during his Farewell Pilgrimage. Ali had been very strict in the sharing out of the booty and his behaviour had aroused protests; doubt was cast on his rectitude, he was reproached with avarice and accused of misuse of authority. Thus it is quite possible that, in order to put an end to all these accusations, Muhammad wished to demonstrate publicly his esteem and love for Ali. Ibn Kathir must have arrived at the same conclusion, for he does not forget to add that the Prophet's words put an end to the murmurings against Ali."

In the Bibliography Mr. Vaglieri writes:

> "According to Ibn Kathir, Muhammad's discourse is reported also by al-Nasa'i in his Sunan and in his book on the khasais of Ali, by Ibn Maja, Abu Dawud and al-Tir-

midhi." On Ali's behaviour during the expedition: to the Yemen: Ibn Hisham 947 f.; Wakidi-Wellhausen, 418; Tubari, i, 1752 f.; Ibn al-Athir, Usd, 27f.; Caetani, Annali, 10 A.H., s17 17 (p. 322)."

After reading the above mentioned historical version of the affair of Ghadir-e-Khom and after knowing that the version has support from other authors and historians, one can form an informed unbiased opinion.

However, there would be some readers who would like to believe, in spite of all the unanswered questions and lack of evidence, that Ali was appointed as The Supreme Authority by Allah's Command at Ghadir-e-Khom. Their false vanity would prevent them from believing otherwise. It is said: "Vanity dies hard, in some obstinate cases it outlives the man". To these self-conceited believers there is one final question. How and from where do you get the knowledge that Ali was also given the power and prerogative of **redelegating** 'The Supreme Authority' to anyone of his male issue? A King's son can be the next King but can a Prime Minister's son inherit the Premiership by the virtue of being a male descendant? Can an entrusted (appointed) authority be bequeathed, generation after generation, like personal wealth? If you have no knowledge or specific information on the subject of redelegation of Authority then what should you do? Allah says:

> "(O man), follow not that whereof thou hast no knowledge. Lo! the hearing and the sight and the heart – of each of these (who follow) it will be asked (on the Day of Reckoning)".
>
> *Holy Quran 17/36*

However, if they choose to follow their own vanities and self esteem after being made aware that the evidence and arguments for what they have been claiming are unfavourable, their false pride will lead them to an unfavourable end. Allah says:

> "Say; 'Enough is Allah for a witness between me and you. He knows what is in the heavens and on earth. And it is those who believe in vanities and reject Allah, that will perish (in the end)".
>
> *Holy Quran 29/52*

6

Unique Legends

History of ancient religions is full of legends, handed down by traditions from earlier times, mostly concerning deities and demigods. Some of the Prophets that came before the advent of Islam performed acts that can be described as supernatural or divine. The Quran acknowledges some of these miracles. However, it also tells us that the men of these times, in spite of witnessing those supernatural happenings, persecuted and in some instances executed their Prophets. The witnessing of the miracles alone was not sufficient for those generations of the sceptical human race to have had a change of heart. The question, therefore is, can the unverifiable legends that speak of divine acts performed centuries ago by Imams or Pirs make anyone a true Muslim?

Prophet Mohammad (s.a.s.) did not perform any major miracle of paramount consequence, during his lifetime. Islam was not spread on the back of miracles. There may be some reported sayings and legends of his miracles, but none has been attested to by the Quran. The foundation of Islam is the Signs of Allah, revealed in the Quran. These Signs are the ever enduring perpetual portents and miracles, for those who are knowledgeable in these *Aayahs* (Signs).

At the other extreme of the sceptical are the people who are undoubting and ready to believe and trust in everything and everyone, in the name of God and religion. Their loyalty is to the Prophets, Imams or Pirs (such as Jesus, Ali or Shams) to whom the divine or supernatural acts are ascribed by legends, and not to Allah who, even if He may be regarded as the ultimate power, is subordinated or held at parity with these individuals, in actual religious practice. In their beseechments, an expectancy of the response is not from Allah, who was in fact glorified by these personalities, but from the venerated Prophets, Imams or Pirs.

A true Muslim is one who expresses loyalty and submits himself to Allah alone; *shirk*, the practice of deifying or in any way treating as Allah's partner or associate any other being, is the most heinous of sins. Even the Holy Prophet, whose deeds and practices are followed by Muslims as best practice – *Sunnah*, is regarded as a mere creation of Allah with no powers but those of a messenger which Allah bestowed on him. He can be praised, but never worshipped as a divine associate or partner of Allah. That is why no Muslim will permit himself to be called a "Mohammedan". The following extract from "The Religions of Man", a book by Huston Smith who is a (non-Muslim) Professor of Philosophy at Washington University, describes adequately how the Holy Prophet saw his role as God's messenger:

> "In an age charged with supernaturalism,
> when miracles were accepted as the stock-

in-trade of the most ordinary saint, Muhammed refused to traffic with human weakness and credulity. To miracle-hungry idolators seeking signs and portents he cut the issue clean: "God has not sent me to work wonders; He has sent me to preach to you. My Lord be praised! Am I more than a man sent as an apostle?" From first to last he resisted every impulse to glamorize his own person. "I never said that Allah's treasures are in my hand, that I knew the hidden things, or that I was an angel . . . I am only a preacher of God's words, the bringer of God's message to mankind." If signs be sought, let them be not of Muhammed's greatness but of God's, and for these one need only open one's eyes. The heavenly bodies holding their swift silent course in the vault of heaven, the incredible order of the universe, the rain that falls to relieve the parched earth, palms bending with golden fruit, ships that glide across the seas laden with goodness for man – can these be the handwork of gods of stone? What fools to cry for signs when creation harbors nothing else! In an age of credulity, Muhammed taught respect for the world's incontrovertible order which was to awaken Muslim science before Christian. Only one miracle is claimed, that of the Koran itself. That he by his own devices could have produced such truth – this was the one naturalistic hypothesis he could not accept."

"The Religions of Man"
page 198 – Harper & Row 1985

In the Ismaili Tariqah, Ginans by Pirs, Farmans by Imams, and history books and religious literature produced by Ismaili writers and Ismailia Associations, are all filled with numerous tales of miracles. Ismaili Imams have positively endorsed these accounts by citing them as evidence of the power of past Imams, and hence of their own.

"Noorum-Mubin" is a voluminous book of the history of 50 Ismaili Pirs and 49 Ismaili Imams. It was written by A.J. Chunara and first published in 1936 by the Press Department of an Aga Khan religious institution called "Recreation Club", Bombay, India (later the Ismailia Association). It has since been revised and reprinted many times. It contains numerous tales of supernatural feats performed by Ismaili Imams and Pirs. This book was recommended as "a must" for his Jamat by Aga Khan III, and the apocryphal Unique Legends it records are accordingly popularly accepted by Ismailis as their official history.

In April 1975, Aga Khan IV, the 49th Imam of Ismailis, passed the undermentioned Resolutions at the Ismailia Association Conference in Paris which he chaired:

Resolution No.3.3.1   "The Nooran Mubeen no longer to be made available to the Jamat as a standard text book of Ismaili history."

Resolution No.3.3.2   "Notwithstanding the above, the Nooran Mubeen to remain as a document for research purposes."

A history of Ismaili Imams and Pirs highly recommended by the 48th Imam in 1936 was thereby withdrawn from circulation by the 49th Imam, within 40 years of its publication.

Another revision of the official position of Ismailis on critical literature concerns the Holy Quran itself, a book 1400 years old and ever in its original form. In 1899, the 48th Imam spoke of it as "1300 years old", "outdated" and "for people of Arabia only"; in October 1986, his successor declared over a television interview: "The only miracle which you have in Islam is the Quran". One must then wonder how matters as fundamental as the importance of the Quran could be the subject of such a radical change of opinion by the infallible and continuous Noor of Imamat!

Going through the history of Ismaili Pirs I have found more legends ascribed to Pir Shamshuddi'n (popularly known as Pir Shams) than to any other Pir. Out of the dozen or so recorded, below are brief accounts of a few, the detailed accounts of which are recorded by A.J. Chunara in "Noorum-Mubin" (Gujrati), and in part by Abualy in "A Brief History of Ismailism" under the chapters 'Imam Shamshuddin Muhammad', 'Imam Kassam Shah' and 'Pir Shamsuddin', respectively.

Unique Legends of Pir Shams

1. Pir Shams had come to the city of Multan, Punjab, Pakistan (formerly India). The king's only son had died recently. The Pir was solicited by Sufis, Alims and others to revive his dead son. Pir Shams approached the dead body, looked at the corpse and said *"Kum be iznillah"* ("Get up by the command of Allah"). The corpse remained stiff and motionless. Then the Pir said *"Kum be izni"* ("Get up by my command") and the king's son got up and was alive.

    Note: Is the Unique Legend trying to propagate that the Pir's command had greater power than that of Allah *(Nauzbillah)*.

The Sufis, Alims and Maulvis of Multan who witnessed the miracle accused the Pir of breaking the law of Shariyat by commanding *"Kum be izni"*. They pronounced that Pir Shams be skinned alive. Thereupon the Pir pulled the locks of his hair and along with it came the skin of his entire body.

2. Pir Shams was very hungry. With difficulty, he could obtain a piece of meat from a butcher. No one in the city of Multan would co-operate with the Pir to cook the meat for him. Pir Shams went out of the city, sat down, looked at the sun (*'Shams'* in Arabic means sun) in the sky and recited a poem in Persian, inviting *'Shams'* (sun) to come down to Pir Shams: "O Sun, O Sun, Do not speed, Do not speed . . . ". Noorum-Mubin records that the sun came down. The entire population of Multan was in pain. Many of them came running to the Pir (who was outside the City) and begged forgiveness. The sun went back to its place in the sky, after cooking the piece of meat.

   Note: No comment is warranted. This is a space era. Everyone can imagine the consequences of the sun stopping in its motion and getting out of its orbit.

3. In the words of author Abualy: "One day Pir Shams sailed in a small boat made of ordinary paper without the boat absorbing water. Thousands of amazed spectators followed the boat walking on both the banks of the river which narrowed upon entering the city. There was a huge building on the right bank where Shaikh Zakaria was living. He saw the Pir through a narrow window of his house and shouted in a curse. Instantly the boat absorbed water and started rolling in rocking motions. The Pir understood his malice and replied, "Let there be horns on thy head", and there appeared instantly two large cow-like horns on Zakaria's head preventing him from

withdrawing his head from outside the window. The Pir corrected his boat and happily sailed away. The frightened Shaikh sent his son and prominent disciples with gifts begging the Pir's forgiveness. He was forgiven conditionally. He would have to keep away from any more mischief. Horns would disappear but as a mark of remembrance he would retain, and his generations would be born with, two small projections on their upper foreheads like those of a kid or a calf".

Note: The same legend appears in an Ismaili Ginan. The name of the Shaikh mentioned in the Ginan is Bahuddin. The correct name of the person is Shaikh Baha'oddin Zakariya Multani, who died in 1276.

It is very interesting to note what author Abualy has added after this legend of the Pir's miracles. He writes **"Even today,** after nearly eight centuries, hundreds of the children of the Shaikh in Multan and the surrounding districts have these projections from birth".

Note: As a resident of Pakistan, for over a quarter century, none of the Ismailis or Muslims of Multan that I had the opportunity of talking to had heard of any clan, tribe, race or family having horn-like projections on their upper foreheads. The book of Abualy was published in 1985 and the words "Even today" indicate that hundreds of individuals with kid or calf like projections are living and can be seen in the district of Multan, Pakistan.

In the following chapters, readers will be interested to learn that the so called "Pir" Shams was neither an Ismaili, nor a "Pir" of the Ismailis. He was not sent to India by a post-Alamut Imam as claimed by Ismaili sources because he arrived in Multan **half a century**

before the destruction of Alamut by the invading Mongolian army of Halaku Khan in 1258 A.D.

Unique Legends of Hazrat Ali

In a small town of Manjewdi, India, on the 29th day of December 1893, Aga Sultan Muhammad Shah, the 48th Imam of Ismailis (Aga Khan III), narrated before the congregation of his followers, an important historical event from the life of Hazrat Ali, the first Ismaili Imam. Reproduced below is the translation thereof:

> "One day Hazarat Amirul Momneen Mawla Murtaza Ali went to a bank of the river Furat, riding his horse", said the Aga Sultan Muhammad. "Ali reached a community of 'Ali Allah'. Members of the community believed Murtaza Ali to be Allah", continued the Aga Khan. "Ali called one member of the community and enquired: 'Do you say Ali Allah?'. The member replied: 'I have faith, you are Allah', (nauzbillah). Thereupon, Ali beheaded him and brought him back to life and asked: 'Why do you call me Ali Allah?'. The member replied: 'You killed me and then brought me back to life, now whatever doubt I had has been thrown out. You are truly Ali Allah'. Murtaza Ali ordered that the person be cut into pieces and thrown from the mountain. The order of Ali was carried out. He was again brought back to life by Ali and asked: 'Do you still call me Ali Allah?'. Thereupon the person very obediently replied: 'My faith has become stronger on the one who can cut a person into pieces and then bring him back to life".

Continuing the narration, Aga Khan said to his Jamat: "The member was killed many times and in many styles and every time brought back to life and asked: 'Do you yet call me Ali Allah?' and the person kept on saying: 'You are truly Allah. The one who kills and gives life be called Allah".
"Kalam e Imam e Mubin" Farman No. 18

Earlier, on the 8th day of September, 1885 Aga Khan had narrated the same miracle of Hazrat Ali in Bombay. In this Farman, he had mentioned the name of the person killed and brought back to life as "Nuseri". The number of times he was killed by Hazrat Ali was mentioned to be seventy. After the narration of the incident, Aga Khan added in his Farman:

"Thereafter came a Commandment that this (Nuseri) is a **True Momin**, and his progenies will also be of such truthfulness. This Momin and his progeny will be exempt from questioning on the Day of Reckoning. He achieved that status because of his *Iman* (faith)". Later on, Aga Khan added "We, the Noor of Murtaza Ali, are present and are sitting in front of you, the Jamat".
"Kalam e Imam e Mubin" Farman No. 2

On page 124 of 'Ismaili Tariqah', Al-Waiz Abualy writes (quoting a portion from Farman No. 2):

"Ismailis believe that every Imam, generation after generation, possesses the same Noor which Ali possessed, therefore **every Imam is Ali**. It is the physical body which is changed, like a dress, but the Noor is perpetual."

Note: According to the above quotation, Ismailis believe **'Ali = Aga Khan'**. If an Ismaili's faith was that of Nuseri or if he happens to be or claims to be a *True Momin* (true believer) like Nuseri, then he must admit without doubt **"Aga Khan = Allah"**, *(nauzbillah)*.

In the town of Mundra, Cutchh, India, on the 21st day of November 1903, eighteen years after the above narration, Aga Khan III narrated another historical event from the life of Hazrat Ali depicting him as 'Ali Allah'. This time Hazrat Ali replies:

> "You are a foreigner from Yemen and yet your faith in me (as Allah) is so complete. You are therefore with me. But, if you were to be with me physically, day and night, and yet had no faith in me, you would be away from me".
>
> Thereafter Aga Khan added, commanding his Jamat: "All you members of the Jamat, **make a firm committment** with your heart that you too are with me. We are with you".
>
> *"Kalam* e *Imam* e *Mubin"* , *Farman No. 80*

Is Divinity a Yo-Yo?

In the year 1945, Aga Khan III made a complete turn about. Having quoted "verbatim" – the conversations between Hazrat Ali and Nuseri – Aga Khan told his missionaries at a Mission Conference in Dar-es-salaam, Africa, that the Supernatural Acts of Hazrat Ali (bringing back to life) "should be considered and interpreted purely as allegoricals." The Legends of Ali, which were narrated in great detail in 1893 and subsequently recorded in the books of Farmans as historical events that actually took place on a bank of river Furat, were so transformed by his own words into allegorical myths (i.e., inventions)!

> Allah says: "Say: Is there of your partners (whom ye ascribe unto Allah) one that leadeth to the Truth? Say: Allah leadeth to the Truth. Is He who leadeth to the Truth more deserving that He should be followed, or he who findeth not the way unless he (himself) be guided. What is the matter with ye? How judge ye? Most of them follow naught but conjecture. Assuredly conjecture can by no means take the place of truth. Verily Allah is well aware of all that they do".
>
> *Holy Quran 10/35-36*

There is one fundamentally important fact which cannot be overlooked and that is:–

Irrespective of the actuality of the supernatural deed of Hazrat Ali (whether it was a historical fact, myth, allegory or fiction), the unvarying, consistent message of these Farmans is the Imam's commandment to his followers to have total faith in him as 'Ali Allah'. The question then is: **Was he or was he not "Ali Allah"?** If he was, then why is his successor, the 49th Imam, denying the Divinity of the Imams? If he was not, then why did the old Aga Khan ask the Jamat to make a firm committment with their hearts and have total faith in him as *"Ali Allah"*?

Is Divinity a toy like a yo-yo which can be spun out for half a century and then reeled in by a string, tied to the finger of an Imam? Ismailis often taunt other Muslims that they (the Muslims) have a 'Mute Quran' which is rigid and cannot change itself with the times. We

Ismailis on the other hand, they say, have a 'Speaking Quran' which changes with the times.

Let us examine the end results:

a) 'Confession of Faith' *(Shahadah)* of Muslims has remained unchanged for the last 1400 years.
b) 'Confession of Faith' of Ismailis has changed twice during the last fifty years and yet the Arabic text of *'Shahadah'* and the official translation do not coincide.

a) The basic text of the *Namaz* (Salat of Muslims) has remained unchanged for the last 1400 years.
b) The text of *Dua* (Salat of Ismailis) and its language has changed three times in the last fifty years and yet there are many self-contradictory, paradoxical phrases in it.

a) The verses of the Quran have not been edited or withdrawn from circulation during the last 1400 years.
b) The Farmans of the 48th Imam were systematically edited and withdrawn from circulation, for various reasons. Many were edited for being contradictory or unfounded or the predictions had gone wrong during his lifetime or after. Today, the Farmans of Aga Khan I, II and III, whether in manuscript, printed or in any form, are recalled by Resolution No. 6.2.4 of the Ismailia Association's Paris Conference, 1975.

According to the Quran, the characteristic portent of Allah's Farman is: "... There is no changing the words of Allah — that is the Supreme Triumph."

Holy Quran 10/64

Hundreds of letters, memorandums and appeals have been sent to Karim Aga Khan by Ismailis, directly to his residence in Aiglemont, France as well as through the Ismailia Councils the world over, seeking guidances on the subject of faith and traditions. Hardly anyone gets an answer or an acknowledgement from Aga Khan, the "Living Guide" and "Speaking Quran" of Ismailis. As for face to face discussion of contentious issues, an Ismaili cannot have that in this life – perhaps in the hereafter?

The 49th Imam has declared through High Courts of London that his grandfather, the 48th Imam, had never claimed Divinity. Did he then not know of the above quoted Farmans made by his grandfather? The books of Farmans are written in the *Khojki* and *Gujrati* languages which the 49th Imam cannot read, so an Ismaili might say *"it is an honest mistake"*. If however, he believes that, then he should ask himself: "How would the 49th Imam know of Ismailis' *'Tasbihs'* and prayers for forgiveness? And how would he know who has paid his contribution of *Dasond* (Ismaili Zakat) in the Jamatkhanas?" No receipt is given for the contribution of Dasond, nor is a list made by the agent of the Imam who collects it and puts it in a bag without counting.

I cannot conclude this chapter without asking: Did Hazrat Ali himself make a claim for being 'Ali Allah', during his lifetime? The answer is found in a letter written by Hazrat Ali, long after having been declared *Mawla* by the Prophet. He wrote the letter before he proceeded to Basra, to fight the battle of Jummal. The letter was addressed to Kufiyites who were leaders of Ansars. His letter begins:

"This letter is from **the servant and creature of God**, Ali . . ."

The full text of the letter appears in "Nahjul Balagha" on page 427.

Allah says:

> "He knoweth what is before them and what is behind them, and they cannot intercede except for him whom He accepteth, and they stand in awe and reverence of His (glory). And one of them who should say: **"Lo! I am a God beside Him"**, that one We should repay with hell. Thus We repay wrongdoers."
>
> *Holy Quran 21/28-29*

As for the sudden lurch and confusion created in the hearts and minds of Ismailis by the duality of Farmans on the subjects of the status of the Quran and the Divinity of the Imam, Allah says:

> "Who is more unjust than one who invents a lie against Allah or rejects His Signs? For such, their portion appointed must reach them from the Book (of Decrees); Until, when Our messengers (of death) arrive and take their souls, they say: **'Where (now) is that to which ye used to invoke besides Allah?'** They will reply, **'They have left us in the lurch'**, And they will bear witness against themselves, that they had rejected Allah."
>
> *Holy Quran 7/37*

7

Unique Statesmanship

Am I not better than a cow?

A high ranking Jamati leader from West Bengal who was on intimate terms with Aga Khan III remarked that many members of the *Jamat* (Community) regarded him as God, and asked if he was. It is reported that Aga Khan quickly and calmly replied that in India millions of people worship cows as their God. Was he not better than a cow? Many years later, the same Jamati leader was in Switzerland and again raised the subject of Divinity and forgiving of sins.

This time the respondent was the grandson of Aga Khan III. Like his predecessor, he came up with a diplomatic counter question: 'What do you believe me to be?'

The man from Calcutta was not an orthodox Ismaili. He used to recite *Namaz*, five times a day. He knew Allah alone can forgive sins. He informed Karim Aga Khan, what he considered him to be. Thereupon the Aga Khan replied: 'That's good enough for me.' The shrewd business magnate knew he was talking to a seasoned statesman, though much younger in age than him.

In a not very distant past, a Chief *Mikhi* (official representative of the Aga Khan) got a *Mulaqat* (audience) with Karim Aga Khan, after much influencing and persuasions. His problem was created by missionaries making sermons in his jurisdictions about Aga Khan's 'Total Divinity'. He wanted to know from his *Hazar Imam* (living guide) what his response should be as a representative of the Imam, especially when confronted by students who had studied Islam or read the Quran. He got back a diplomatic counter question: 'Who are those missionaries?'

Karim Aga Khan was on his tour of Uganda, East Africa. He happened to visit an Aga Khan School in Kampla. One of the students of the Aga Khan School got up and asked the visitor a point-blank question; **"Are you God?"** Aga Khan turned around and asked the Educational Administrator for the Aga Khan Schools, who was also an Ismaili, to answer that question. Obviously, any answer given by the Administrator would only qualify as his own personal belief and not a response from Aga Khan. On his way back, he inquired who is teaching students that he is God?

"The only miracle in Islam is the Quran"

This time Aga Khan was on television. It is reported that Aga Khan had refused offers from leading American Television Corporations for an interview. Katherine

Smalley, a producer for C.B.C., Toronto and famous interviewer Roy Bonnisteel were lucky enough to have Aga Khan on their popular program 'Man Alive'. After a series of questions, Roy touched the sensitive nerve of His Highness. He asked, "Is this a kind of Divine authority?" Every Ismaili viewer on that night of October 8, 1986 was tense. The question was straight forward and direct. The viewers were expecting a simple 'Yes' or 'No'. Instead, Aga Khan's response was, not to confuse the concept of 'Religious Authority' with Divinity. He said: "The Prophet himself never claimed any miracle of any sort. The only miracle which you have in Islam is the Quran".

Conferences and Conclusions

I was sitting in a conference room of a hotel on the outskirts of Paris. I was not sure what would be the reaction from the Chair on that day. The night before, in the shivering cold of October, I had prepared my paper for the next day's presentation. The moment came and Aga Khan asked me to read my paper, which was titled; *"God is out of fashion in the West – says Pope"*. The stress point of the paper was, if that be the case then what should be the approach of our young and old missionaries towards the coming generations since people of the third world eventually do catch up with the West. During the discussions, a President of the Ismailia Association brought up the subject of sermons delivered on 'Divinity'. He addressed the Chair drawing attention to an incident that had taken place a short time ago, which was as follows: A Senior *Al-Waiz* (missionary) had come on a visit to Pakistan. He is reputed for his sermons on "Ali *sahi* (truly) Allah", that is to say "Aga Khan is truly Allah". The visiting missionary had scheduled his program for lectures and sermons without going through the official channel. The President of the Ismailia Association who was himself a missionary, instructed the Jamati Officers to cancel the program. The Senior missionary knew that in Pakistan the Ismailia Association would not allow him to preach what he propagated outside of Pakistan. He therefore decided to by-pass the Association and change the venue of his lectures. The sermons were now to be delivered outside of a Jamatkhana in Karachi.

The said Jamatkhana is located within a huge housing complex for Ismailis. The Housing Society is owned by a Charitable Trust. *Mukhis* who were directly responsible to the Association had no jurisdiction outside of their Jamatkhanas. This could create even greater problems than before because the entrance to the complex was not restricted to the Ismailis only as Jamatkhana entrances.

The Federal Council for Pakistan appointed me as mediator, being a President of the Regional Council for Karachi and Baluchistan. Finally, permission was granted to the visiting missionary for delivering sermons in all the Jamatkhanas of Karachi. The visitor made good of the opportunity granted and left Pakistan, leaving behind a legacy of questions and problems for the local missionaries and the Ismailia Association.

In Pakistan, *"Islamiyat"* (relating to Islam) is a compulsory subject, in the secular schools at the elementary and secondary levels. Every student living in Pakistan is familiar with the fundamental principles of Islam, Islamic history and the basic Message of the Quran. One can well imagine the plight of the President of the Association who addressed the Chair at the Conference in Paris, following the sermons by the visiting missionary. The object of my paper that day, and that of the President's remark were to have a definitive guideline from the Chair (Aga Khan) about missionaries' approach to the subject of "Ali Allah" and 'Divinity'.

In the past, Aga Khan was inquiring as to "Who are these missionaries?" Now a missionary was identified and Aga Khan was also informed, by his own appointee (the President) as to the dominating power of that missionary. All delegates attending the conference were expecting a strong response and a positive reaction from the Chair. The chair-person calmly suggested that the issue be left with him. Karim Aga Khan did not advise the delegates what to do in the future, if the Senior missionary or any other preacher came to Pakistan and wanted to preach "Ali sahi Allah".

Many years later, I met the Senior Al-Waiz in Canada. He laughed and said; 'I know what happened on that day at the Conference in Paris'. His laughs told me the untold story. It was not difficult to read between the lines or rather, between the lips.

Today, 15 years have passed since that Conference in 1973. The Senior missionary and his colleagues are harping the same old tune. He goes a step further by propagating *"Sahi Allah"* (true God), for not only Karim Aga Khan, but also for Hazrat Ali, Prophet Muhammad, Hazrat Bibi Fatima, Hazrat Hasan and Hazrat Hussain who are know as *"Punjtan Pak'* (five holy bodies). *(nauzbillah)*

Memorandums and Mulaqats

In 1985, I prepared a "Memorandum" for submission to Aga Khan IV. The main issue of the memorandum was about 'Resolutions' that were passed at a top level conference and then swept under the rug by a group of

Canadian leaders and missionaries. The subjects for the memorandum and the object of submitting it were already discussed at a gathering attended by a few leaders from the Council, the Associations and the Jamat. A high-ranking leader of the Canadian Jamat undertook to deliver the memorandum to Aga Khan personally. Since the issues were dividing the leaders, scholars, missionaries and members of the Jamat, an audience was requested with Aga Khan during his visit of Vancouver.

Shortly after, Aga Khan came to Vancouver and I was invited to a private gathering in West Vancouver to have a *Mulaqat* (audience) with Karim Aga Khan and discuss the topics of the memorandum submitted earlier. The President who had been very co-operative and friendly, introduced me to Aga Khan. I shook his hand and said: "Your Highness, I would like to have a Mulaqat with you". He petted my shoulder with his left hand and said: "Your family has done a great service in India" and extended his right hand to the person next in the line for introduction. Aiglemont (Aga Khan's office in France), has a big file of my family and me.

These days, it is hard to know what is in fashion and what is out of fashion in the Ismaili Tariqah.

> "The day He will gather them together as well as those whom they worship besides Allah. He will ask:"Was it you who led these My servants astray, or did they stray from the Path themselves?
>
> *Holy Quran 25/17*

8

Unique Ginans

Ginans – (Devotional Songs in Indian languages) are the basis and foundation of the Ismaili Tariqah. Forefathers of the present day Khoja Ismailis were converted by Pirs from Hinduism with the Ginanic preachings. Divine Revelations, revealed unto mankind through Prophet Muhammad by Allah, are the basis and foundation of Islam. Disputing the preachings of the Ginans by an Ismaili Momin would be similar in significance to the contradiction of the teachings of the Quran by a believing Muslim. Any study of the Ismaili Tariqah, without the study of the origins of Ginans and their influence upon Ismailis, would be an incomplete study.

"Pir" is a Persian word. It means *Murshid, Guru,* an authorized teacher. To an Ismaili, the teachings of a Pir are to be obeyed, word for word. Author Abualy has quoted a *Farman* (Command) of an Imam on Page 134 of 'Ismaili Tariqah' to show that the obedience to Pir is obligatory upon every Ismaili. The quoted Farman reads:

> "The Pir is the person to whom the Imam of the time has granted his position which makes him the highest amongst his creation *(ashraf-i-makhluqat)* and whenever the Imam has chosen the Pir and appointed him, he must convey to others the knowledge in detail. You must attain perfection in the knowledge of the Imam through him. Therefore it is obligatory upon you to follow the Pir, never flinching from his obedience. Be bound by what the Pir tells you, acting as he says and when you obey the Pir, the Pir in the Hereafter, will pray to God for your protection".

More Ginans Composed by non-Pirs than Pirs

Ismailis recite Ginans everyday with love and devotion in their Jamatkhanas, but most Ismailis have not studied the history and origin of these Ginans. They believe that each and every Ginan that is recited in their Jamatkhanas and/or published by the Ismailia Association is composed by an authorized Pir and must be obeyed. However, that is not so. In fact, **there are more Ginans composed by non-Pirs than there are by Pirs.** Author Abualy writes on pages 134 and 135 of his book 'Ismaili Tariqah':-

> "The children of our Holy Pirs were also respectfully called Pirs. They were not the

Appointed Pirs as *Hujjatul Imam* but they were dais, missionaries. They were Sayyids ... **There is nothing wrong to call these children of our Holy Pirs as Pirs** ... Our Pirs and their children composed the Ginans in various Indian languages. **The present collection of our Ginanic literature is the work of our ten Appointed Pirs and more than twenty of their children.** Bhagat Kara Ruda said that more than forty Sayyids among the children of our Holy Pirs, particularly **the children of Pir Sadruddin and Pir Hasan Kabirdin, had composed thousands of Ginans,** most of which were lost with time".

The amazing statement in the fourth sentence surely leads to these questions:

1. Is there anything wrong then in addressing children of our Holy Imams, also respectfully, as Imams?

2. Admitted, they are not Appointed Imams like our Hazar Imam. But, should not the spoken words of these children of Imams be considered as Farmans and obeyed, word for word, like the Ginans created by the children of our Appointed Pirs?

Ginans - Creations of anonymous authors!

Professor W. Ivanow, a well known Russian scholar and a reputed researcher of Ismaili history, has translated many books and manuscripts of Ismaili literature.

He writes in his book 'Ismaili Literature' (Tehran University Press - 1963):-

> "A great majority of *gnans* are the creation of anonymous authors. Apparently quite a considerable proportion of those attributed to the authorship of Great Pirs **probably have nothing to do with them, and were composed at a much later date.** This particularly applies to the gnans about various Pirs, their miracles, their sayings". (Page 174)

Hundreds of Ginans which were composed by the children and grandchildren of the Pirs were attributed to Pir Sadruddin and Pir Hasan Kabirdin by these descendants. Writing new Ginans and selling them to newly converted Khojas was the main source of income for these hundreds of relatives of Pirs. Ismailia Association for India has confirmed these facts and added that "out of 18 sons of Pir Hasan Kabirdin, 17 sons had opened various religious Bazaars of their own and had started their own independent factories "ગઈ ગઈ". Some of these so called Sayyids had even established their own sects.

In 1969, the Ismailia Association for India published a series of "Collection of Ginans" (2nd edition). This series includes Ginans composed by officially appointed authorized Pirs, Ginans by *Sayyids* (descendants of the Pirs) whose names and brief history are published in the introduction, and also Ginans composed by so called Sayyids, whose historical record is neither available nor known.

Below are three excerpts from the introductions of this series published from Bombay, India by the Ismailia Association:-

1. સત્તાધારી પીરો ઉપરાંત પીરોના અમુક વંશજોએ પણ પોતાના બાપદાદાના પંથ ઉપર કાયમ રહી દઆવતનું કાર્ય ચાલુ રાખ્યું હતું જેમણે કેટલાક ગીનાનો રચ્યા છે, જેમાં ગૈયદ ઇમામશાહનો મોટો હિસ્સો છે.

2. એટલું ધ્યાનમાં રાખવું જોઇએ કે અનેક ઇસમાઇલી કવીઓ અને ફિલસુફો અને ભકતોએ કાવ્યો રચી ઇસમાઇલી સત્પંથનો બોધ કર્યો છે, તેમ સૈયદોએ જે બોધ કર્યો અને ગીનાનો રચ્યા તે આપણા ધાર્મિક સાહિત્યમાં જળવાઇ રહેલ છે. તેમાં રહેલો બોધ જ આપણે ગ્રહણ કરવાનો છે. પણ તેમના ગીનાનોને ઇમામે ઝમાન તરફથી નિમાયેત્ર સત્તાધારી પીરોના ગીનાનો જેટલું વજન આપી શકાય નહિ

3. વળી એ બધા શાસ્ત્રોના મૂળ કર્તા કોણ? એ સવાલને છણતાં એ દેખાઇ આવે છે કે કેટલાક સૈયદોએ મૂળ પીરોના જ્ઞાન કે શાસ્ત્રોમાં પોતાના નામો ઉમેરી દીધા હોય એ પણ બનવા યોગ્ય છે.

Translation of the above excerpts:

1. Besides the authorized Pirs, descendants of the Pirs have also propagated faith in the same manner as their fathers and grandfathers. These descendants have composed some Ginans in which Sayyid Imamshah's contribution is the greatest.

2. It should be borne in mind (by Ismailis) that **many Ismaili Poets, Philosophers and Bhagats** *(devouts)* have written songs and propagated the true path of Ismailism. Similarly, Sayyids (and one Sayyidah) have also composed Ginans and propagated the faith. These compositions have been preserved in our religious literature. We have only to adopt the preachings that are within these compositions (Ginans). But, the Ginans of these composers cannot be given the same **"weight"** as those composed by the authorized Pirs that were nominated by Imam-e-Zaman.

3. Who were the original creators (composers) of all these sacred writings (Ginans)? In trying to find an answer to this question it is being observed that it is likely that some *Sayyids* (descendants of Pirs) might have added their names to the original Ginans or sacred writings created by Pirs.

It is evident from the last excerpt that the Ismailia Association is trying to impress upon Ismailis that although a Ginan may mention the name of a Sayyid or Sayyidah as the composer, it could be a composition of an authorized Pir. In other words, it should be given the same "weight" as an authorized composition.

The collection of "Ginans" published by the Ismailia Association for India is made from the following categories:–

1. Authorized Ginans composed by appointed Pirs.

2. Devotional Songs composed by *known* Sayyids.

3. Devotional Songs composed by *unknown* Sayyids.

Ginans and songs are both **officially called Ginans.** Both are being equally honoured, trusted and obeyed by Ismailis, because they bear the same nomenclature. In some cases the name of a father appears as the creator Pir and his son's name appears, in the same verse, as the reciter Pir. There are even cases where the prefix 'Pir' is added to the name of the composer when he is neither a Pir, nor a descendant of any Pir or Sayyid. Below is one such **"Phony Ginan"** created during my lifetime.

Who wrote "Par karo beda Guruji"?

A Ginan which begins with "Par karo beda Guruji" is often being recited in the Jamatkhanas of Canada. It is a "song" composed by Head Master (Head Teacher) Hussain Gulamhussain Hussaini of a religious night school at Khadak, Bombay, India in the 1940's. In those days I was one of the teachers in that school. The Head Master had a poetic talent and used to compose songs for students of the night school to sing in the night school *"Majlis"*. Later on, this particular song became a "Ginan". Master Hussaini who had composed the song, under the pen-name of *"Musst"* (in high spirits - carefree), became "Pir Musst Musst Hussaini" instead of "Musst Master Hussaini". The majority of Ismailis do not know such historical facts behind the origin of Ismaili Ginans. A missionary would not reveal these facts, in order to preserve the "weight" of Ginanic literature. They want Ismailis to obey each and every "Ginan" with the same respect in spite of the fact that **there are more unauthorized Ginans than there are authorized ones.**

Who wrote "Garbis" of Pir Shams?

Ismaili sources record that Pir Shams was sent to India by one of their Imams from Iran. He was born in Iran. He died in Multan, Pakistan (formerly India). The custodian of the shrine in Multan has a genealogy tree *(Sajrah)* which records that he was born in Gazhni and came from Afghanistan. He was not an Ismaili and he did not propagate the Ismaili faith. However, the point to note is that he was a foreigner when he came to India. History records that he travelled from Afghanistan to Sind, Punjab, Kashmir and Tibet and settled in Multan (Punjab), where he died. Even the Ismaili sources have no records of his stay in Cutchh, Kathiawar or Gujrat where the inhabitants speak Gujrati.

In the Jamatkhanas of Punjab, Ismailis recite Ginans in Punjabi which they say were composed by Pir
Shams, seven centuries ago. In most of the other Jamatkhanas the world over, Ismailis recite *Garbis* (folk
songs in Gujrati to which men and women would dance
at a festival, with music), *Kathas*, *Salokas* and *Ginans*
in Gujrati which they claim were all composed by Pir
Shams. This entire collection in Gujrati language would
be of over 2000 verses.

This gives rise to a series of questions:

1. When and where did Pir Shams learn Gujrati?

2. Why would he compose and sing Ginans in
    Gujrati before his non-Gujrati adherents?

3. Was the art of poetry writing in Gujrati already
    developed 700 years ago?

Examining the standard of the language of the Garbis and Ginans by Pir Shams, one can say that they are
the work of an individual well versed in contemporary
as well as medieval Gujrati.

Who edited "Pir Pandiyat-i Jawan-mardi"?

It is interesting to note that in the Ismaili Tariqah,
one of the "Authorized Pirs" is a "Book". The Book is
supposed to have been written by a Nizari Imam whose
name was Ali, but who has been called Mustansir Billah
II. The Book is called "Pir Pandiyat-i Jawan-mardi" — a
strange name for a Pir. For more details please read
page 123 and 124 of 'A Brief History of Ismailism' by
Abualy A. Aziz.

Professor W. Ivanow translated "Pir Pandiyat-i
Jawan-mardi" into English and published the text of the

work and its translation through 'The Ismaili Society', Bombay, in 1953. Ten years later he wrote:—

"Taking into consideration the fundamental differences between various versions of the text, mentioned in the Introduction, it is easy to suspect that the work (Pandiyat-i Jawan-mardi) has passed through the hands of Khayrkhwah (Herati), who had no scruples about 'editing' it, and probably ultimately it reached India in his version"
'Ismaili Literature' Tehran University Press, 1963. Page 139

Who wrote "Kalam-i Pir"?

Khayrkhwah Herati is also suspected by Professor Ivanow of committing "the worst plagiarism" and converting "Haft-bab-i Bu Ishaq" (Haft-bab written by Abu Ishaq Quhistani) into "Haft-bab-i Shah Sayyid Nasir" (Haft-bab written by Sayyid Nasir-i Khusraw), otherwise known as "Kalam-i Pir". This book is considered 'Pir', by Ismailis of Badakshan and Northern Pakistan. It has also been translated by Professor W. Ivanow into English in 1959.

"Editing" of books written by Pirs and Imams is not an uncommon practice in this Unique Tariqah. The "edited" version is treated with the same veneration and glory as if it was the original unedited version, because an Ismaili cannot distinguish the edited portion from the unedited.

Who were "Khojas"?

Pirs had converted Hindus into Khojas and not into Ismailis. It has been a subject of debate whether the converted Khojas were Shias or Sunnis. History records and 'Noorum Mubin' confirms that prior to the arrival of Aga Khan I, in India from Iran in 1843, all the essential communal ceremonies of the Khojas, such as marriages, deaths, circumcisions, *Fatehas* etc., were being performed by **Sunni Mullahs** as per the traditions of *'Ahle Sunnat'*; showing that the names of Shia Imams were not included in these rituals. 'Noorum Mubin' records that in 1271 A.H. Aga Khan I issued a "circular" to the Khojas asking them to change these ceremonies to *'Shia Tariqah'* and rituals to be performed by Shia Maulvis and Sayyids, instead of Sunni Mullahs. For 20 years, the influencial Jamati members in Cutch and Kathiawar disputed the change and the authority of Aga Khan and his circular. 'Noorum-Mubin' records that a compromise was reached between the disputing Khojas and Aga Khan I. Khojas agreed to abide by the circular except in the matter of marriages, where the Nikah ceremonies would continue to be performed as per 'Sunni Tariqah'.

Slowly the term "Khojas" was phased out and the Khojas became known as "Ismailis" (followers of the 6th generation of Ali, called Ismail), hence followers of Ali (Shias) in their true sense. In North America the name Ismail has often been confused with Ishmael, the eldest son of patriarch Abraham.

For further information please refer to Noorum Mubin pages 438 and 439. Also, a booklet published in 1932 by Universal Printing House, Karachi, written by K. Goolamali, entitled 'An Appeal to Mr. Ali Soloman Khan'. Abualy has recorded a very brief account of the above but the equivalent dates in A.D., recorded by Noorum Mubin and Abualy differ. Noorum Mubin records that 1279 A.H. = 1832 A.D. and 1293 A.H. = 1866 A.D. Abualy records that 1252 A.H. = 1836 A.D. and 1282 A.H. = 1866 A.D.!

Who made "w'Allah" ("By God!"), into Allah?

Over a period of seven centuries, the original Ginans have gone through lots of transitions. Most of the old Ginans have either been lost or removed from circulation permanently. In their places new Ginans have been added. Ginans were composed by Sayyids (male and female) until the last century. Many Ginans have been edited by the Ismailia Associations. Some Ginans are banned by the Imams. Others have been modified or recast to incorporate Shia beliefs or to glorify the image of Ali. For example, the word *"Hari"* has been replaced with "Ali", *"Swami"* is changed to "Sami" and "w'Allah e'hi Imam" meaning "By God! that (Islam Shah) is Imam" has been altered to read "Allah e'hi Imam" meaning "Allah that is (equal to) Imam", *(nauzbillah)*. The texts of some of these Ginans are beyond human reasoning and logic. Yet, in spite of these corruptions, Ginans are the basis of Ismaili beliefs. Ismailis burst with joy and pride when they sing "Allah e'hi Imam" not knowing that they are uttering a blasphemy and committing a heinous sin.

On pages 136 and 137 of 'Ismaili Tariqah' Abualy has quoted nearly a dozen or so Farmans of Aga Khan III on Ginans. Reproduced below are three Farmans:-

> "Pir Sadruddin composed the Ginans, in Indian languages, which are the extracts from the Quran".

> "Pir Sadruddin has given you, in his Ginans, the tafseer (interpretation) of the Quran-e-Shariff".

> "Pir Sadruddin has guided you to the Right Path. If (instead) you will follow the path of the Moguls and the Arabs, you will be lost".

Prophet Muhammad came to India as "Pir"!

On page 133, Abualy has quoted a Ginan of Pir Sadruddin in Gujrati and has given the translation thereof as under:—

એજી પહેલે ખંધુકારમાંહે નથી મુહમ્મદ મુસ્તફા,
સોહી ગુર જંબુદીપ માંહે આયા–એક.

Translation:

> "Before the creation there was Nabi Mohammed Mustafa. The same Murshid has come to India."

Such fantastic claims made in the names of Pirs are the basis of the Ismaili Tariqah's bizarre teachings and beliefs of the repeated incarnations of Hazrat Ali and Nabi Muhammad as the *'Avtaras'* of Hindu deities; *'Vishnu'* and *'Bramah'* respectively, from before the Creation (ખંધુકાર). Ismailis are also taught that the Pirs who came to India were the holders of the Noor of Prophet Muhammad - the *Bramah,* and the Aga Khans are the final *Avtaras of Lord Vishnu.* Rama and Krishna were also Avtaras of Vishnu.

Prophet acknowledged Ali was the Creator!

Quoted below is another "Unique Ginan". The Ginan is published under a collection entitled *"Momin Chetavni".* This Ginan is in connection with the birth of Ali ibn Abu Talib. It narrates a dialogue between Muhammed Mustafa (who was not yet Prophet and was 29 years of age) and a group of Angels who had come down from heaven to see Ali ibn Abu Talib, who had just been born.

એજી તારે સલામ કરી તે તો પાછા વળીઆ,
તે મલાએક ને સરદાર,
તારે મલાએકે નથી મુહંમદને કહ્યું,
એ તો છે અશર્ કુર્ષનો કિરતાર...ચેતો.

એજી અમને જેણે હુકમ કરીઆ,
અને મૂકીઆ તમ પાસે સરદાર;
સોહી અમે એને જાણતા,
તે માંહે શક નહિ રે લગાર....ચેતો.

એજી તારે નથી મુહંમદ એમ બોલીઆ,
ભાઈ મલાએક તમને કહું વિચાર;
અમને પોતે ઓળખાવીઆ,
એ છે સૃષ્ટિનો સર્જનહાર....ચેતો.

Translation:

"When Nabi Muhammed, the leader of the Angels, returned after doing his Salaam (to Ali), the Angels said to Nabi Muhammed "He (Baby Ali) is the creator of 'Arsh Kursh' (Heavenly throne); He (Ali) is the one who has commanded us and kept us under your leadership. He is indeed the same, without any doubt". Then Nabi Muhammed replied "Brother Angels, let me tell you my thoughts; He (Baby Ali) has made known to me, **he is the Creator of this Universe**".

Can these Ginans be considered as the "extracts from the Quran"? Does the Quran speak of "Ali the Creator of this Universe"?

No Muslim in his right mind would believe a single verse of the above Ginans. Any individual (Muslim or non-Muslim) who has read the history of the Great

Prophet of Islam would say that when the Prophet Muhammad heard Angel Jibrael (Gabriel) for the first time in his life, it was in the cave of Mount Hira and he being about 40 years old. If the Prophet at the age of 29 years knew "Ali is the Creator of this Universe" then why did he go to Mount Hira? Why was the Prophet shocked to hear the voice of Angel Jibrael in the cave, if they both had known each other and spoken before? Finally, who told the Pir what the Prophet said to the Angels 700 years ago? Such Ginans are the basis for establishing the "Unique Supremacy" of Ali and his successors, the Aga Khans.

Allah created Adam and gave him wisdom. He implanted in him the faculty of knowledge and judgement, before sending him upon this earth. He also gave him the power of reasoning, intuition and instinctive feelings. He therefore enjoys a special place within the creation of Allah — "Ashraful Makhlukat". Allah has honoured Adam to be His vicegerent on earth — "Khaliful Ardh". We, the human race, inherited these faculties. Today, the sources of acquiring knowledge are unlimited and easily accessible. This makes one wonder why Ismailis of this 20th century, who are so advanced and discerning in managing their financial affairs, become so gullible as to place their entire confidence in Ginans, and base their religious beliefs on such bizarre Ginanic legends of Ali and Nabi and not the Quranic teachings?

> The Quran teaches: "Say, I (Muhammad)
> am no more than a human being like you".
> *Holy Quran 18/10*

As for the supremacy of Hazrat Ali; in the Fatimid period (i.e. pre-Alumut and pre-Ginanic period), Ali was considered as *"al-Wasiyin wa Wazir Khair al-Mursalin"*, meaning "the distinguished Nominee and Representative *(Wazir)* of the Messenger". These words were inscribed on the obverse of the Fatimid Dinars to describe their Imams – the descendants of Ali.

Should not the Aga Khan ask his followers to consider him, *'Wazir of the Messenger'*, since he claims to be a descendant of the Fatimid Imams?

Who are Moguls and Arabs?

Incidentally, there is another Farman of Aga Khan III which speaks of Moguls as being "beggars" and Arabs "like donkeys' and "what will they teach Ismailis?" The Farman is in *"Khojki"* (a script especially developed by Khoja-Ismailis, for private records and secret writings). This Farman was made on August 20, 1899 in Zanzibar, Africa.

Translation:

> "Pir Sadardin has shown you the straight path, if you leave that, and walk upon the talks of Moguls and Arabs, then you will fall down. **Arabs are like donkeys.** What will they teach you? They themselves do

not know anything, then what will they teach you? **Moguls seek alms in every country.** What will they teach you? If you follow their talks, then you too will become donkeys".

(Bahere Rehmat, pages 30 & 31)

Aga Khan III tells Ismailis in the Farman that if they follow the words of Moguls and Arabs they will fall down and become like donkeys. The question is, who was Aga Khan III? Did he not call himself a Hashemite? Who were Hazrat Ali (r.a.) and Nabi Muhammad (s.a.s.)? Finally, **who is Aga Khan IV?** Is he Italian, French, British, Irani or an Arab? He calls himself Karim al-Hussaini. Who were Hashem and Hussain, if not Arabs?

Muslims — those who submit to Allah — have based their religious beliefs by reference to the *"Words of their Creator"* — the Quran. Ismaili Momins — those who submit to their Imams — have based their religious beliefs by reference to the *"words of Poets"* — the Ginans. Which Tariqah is on the right path? Allah says:

"Shall I inform you, (O people!), on whom it is that the evil ones descend? They descend on every lying, wicked person, (into whose ears) they pour hearsay vanities, and most of them are liars. And the **Poets,** — it is those straying in evil, who follow them: Seest thou not that they wander distracted in every valley? And that they say what they practise not?"

Holy Quran 26/221 to 226

9

Unique Du'a

In the Ismaili Tariqah the first Article of Faith is a Declaration of faith, the second is *Baiyat* (oath of allegiance to the Imam) and the third is *Dua* (prayer). In Islam the first article is a Declaration of faith and the second is *Salat* - the canonical daily prayers. In the Persian and Urdu languages they are called *Namaz*.

The Ismaili is enjoined to perform only three obligatory prayers *(Dua)*. The Muslim is enjoined to perform five obligatory prayers *(Namaz)* every day. When possible, prayers must be performed in congregation, especially the Friday noon prayers. In the Ismaili Tariqah there is no noon prayer (Dua) on Friday or any other day.

A Muslim stands before Allah in his Namaz and faces the *Qiblah* (the Holy House of Allah in Mecca). An Ismaili sits in his Dua and faces the photograph of his Hazar Imam. In Islam, the person who leads the congregational prayer *(Pesh Imam)* faces in the same direction as the rest of the congregation. In the Ismaili Tariqah, the person who leads the prayer faces the congregation and the Jamat faces the *Pesh Imam*. They both prostrate facing each other. In the Jamatakhana, any Ismaili boy or girl of any age, a man or a woman, can lead the congregational prayer.

". . . they bow not down!"

A Muslim, be he Sunni or Shia, begins his (or her) Namaz in a standing position. After reciting the verses of the chapter 'the opening' (*al-Fatihah*) and at least three other verses from the Quran, he goes into bowing position (*Ruku*). After Praising and Glorifying the Lord in the Ruku, he resumes the standing position and goes into Prostration (*Sajdah*). An Ismaili recites his (or her) entire Dua in a squatting position, and as such, does not do the *Ruku*.

> "O, ye who believe! Bow down (*Ruku*) and prostrate (*Sujood*) yourselves and worship your Lord and do good that ye may prosper."
> "Woe unto the Rejecters of Truth on that day! and when it is said unto them: Bow down (Ruku), *they bow not down!*"
> *Holy Quran 22/77; 77/47-48*

A Muslim, upon meeting another, would greet him with "Peace be upon you" or "Peace be upon you, and Mercy of Allah, and Prosperity" and he would be reciprocated with a similar greeting. An Ismaili, upon meeting another, would say: *"Ya Ali Madad"* (O Ali, Help) and he would be reciprocated with *"Mawla Ali Madad"* (Our Lord Ali, Help).

The entire Islamic *Ummah* (Brotherhood), including all schools of thought of Sunni and Shia Tariqahs (except Ismailis), recite *"Subaanna Rabbiyal Azeem* (Glory to my Lord the Great) while in Ruku and *"Subhaanna Rabbiyal Aala"* (Glory to my Lord the Highest) in their Sujood. Ismailis do not recite the above two phrases. They glorify Ali and his sword *"Zulfiqar"* in their Dua. They recite *"La fata illa Ali la saifa illa Zulfiqar"* ("There is no Hero except Ali, there is no sword except Zulfiqar"). An individual is meant to be in communication with his Creator in his institutional prayers. Are Ismailis trying to communicate to (i.e. inform) Allah that Ali is the only Hero or Victorious one from amongst His creation and his sword is exceptionally divine?

At the end of their Dua, Ismailis shake hands with the persons (male or female) sitting on either side of them, saying *"Shah-jo-deedar",* meaning "May you have *Deedar* (glimpse) of Shah (Hazar Imam - the Aga Khan)". Whereas, a Muslim worshipper turns his face to the right saying *"Assalamu allai kum wa rahmattu Allah",* meaning "Peace be upon you and Allah's mercy"; and then turns his face to the left saying the same words. Thereafter he raises his hands, seeks forgiveness, etc., etc., and concludes his prayers by reciting "Praise be to Allah, Lord of the worlds".

> "Those who believe and work righteousness, their Lord will guide them because of their faith: Beneath them will flow rivers in Gardens of Bliss. Their prayer therein will be: ***"Glory to thee, O Allah! "*** and their greetings therein will be: Peace. And the conclusion of their prayers will be: Praise be to Allah, Lord of the worlds!"
>
> *Holy Quran 10/9-10*

Double Standards

Reproduced below are a few excerpts from the book of Dua to show the kind of Standards upheld. Addressing Allah, in Part II of Dua, Ismailis recite:–

"Oh Allah, O our Lord, from Thee is my help and upon Thee is my reliance. **Thee alone** we worship and from **Thee alone** we seek help".

Immediately after this, they recite:–

"O Aly, come to my help by Thy favours".

In Part III of Dua, they recite:–

"Seek at the time of difficulty the help of your Lord, the present (Imam) Shah Karim al-Husayni".

There are two points worth noting:–

1. The sincerity and earnestness of **"Thee alone"** expires and vanishes the moment they seek help from Aly, **besides** Allah.

2. The wording of the excerpt from Part III indicates that it is neither a supplication to Allah, nor to Aga Khan. It is like a *command* or a *sermon* to the reciter. And yet, it forms an integral part of a prayer to Allah!

In the fifth part of the *Dua* (ritual prayer), there is a *'Tasbih'* in which Ismailis recite "O Aly, O Muhammad; O Muhammad, O Aly", eleven times. Allah says:

"And the places of worship are only for Allah, so invoke not unto **anyone along with Allah**"

Holy Quran 72/18.

Ismailis recite 'reconstituted' verse in Dua

As a rule, a Muslim would not recite a partial or incomplete verse of the Quran in his (or her) Salat. A Muslim could never imagine that someone would knowingly ask his fellow Muslims, by virtue of his authority, to recite in their daily Salat, the beginning of verse "A" coupled and connected together with the end part of verse "B", from a totally different chapter of the Quran. It would be a great shock for Muslims, as well as for the majority of Ismailis, to learn that Aga Khan has commanded Ismailis to recite such a *"reconstituted"* verse in their daily Dua. The reconstituted verse is an admixture of an incomplete verse 4/59 and an incomplete verse 36/12.

Salat means contact prayer. In his Namaz, a Muslim is expressing his feelings and thoughts to Allah — the Glorious Author of the sacred verses of the Quran. Knowingly interchanging the lines of two verses and connecting the message of one incomplete verse to another incomplete verse whilst reciting the prayer, is to convey to the Author that he knows a better formation or the correct arrangement of the revealed text. To delete the bottom half of the one verse and the top half of the other verse, is to express that he (a Muslim – one who has submitted himself to Allah) is a better editor, and is more knowledgeable to judge and decide what is essential and what is superfluous (*nauzbillah*). Commanding with his authority one million Muslims (Ismailis) to repeat the "reconstituted and edited" verse, three times a day, for a period of over 30 years, is to endorse and establish the *"edited version"* as opposed to the *"Original Text"*. Such an "Edited Salat" is neither a supplication nor a glorification. It is a profanity and sacrilege. Even from a worldly point of view, a similar act of editing and then reconstituting the works of, say, Homer or Milton, would be an act uncondonable by society. It would be a serious affront to these great poets. How great then the affront to Allah?

Two Duas (Pakistani and African)

The old Dua, which is alleged to have been given by Pir Sadruddin, was in Gujrati. In 1956, this was replaced by a new Dua in Arabic. This Dua was formulated and authorized by the Farman of Aga Khan III. It was introduced in Africa by Karim Aga Khan and into the other parts of the world through the Ismailia Associations. In those days I was living in Karachi, Pakistan. The Ismailis of Pakistan were commanded by Aga Khan III to recite in their prostration, *"Allahumma laka sujoodi wa ta'ati"* meaning **"O Allah** to Thee is my prostration and obedience".

I had occasion to visit my parents in Congo, Africa and was surprised to hear the Ismailis of Africa reciting *"al-Imamul haziril maujood li zikrihis sujood"* meaning **"the present Imam,** to whose name prostration is due", instead of the above mentioned phrase being recited in Pakistan. Aga Khan III had devised **two Duas**; one for the Ismailis of the Islamic States and the other for the Ismailis of the non-Islamic States. What a Unique Deception! One could deceive the Government of Pakistan and its citizens, but Allah knows what was in the hearts and what was on the tongues of Ismailis and their Imam.

"Verily Allah is Aware of what is hidden in the breasts"

Holy Quran 39/7

Ismailis of Africa were also commanded by Aga Khan III to say an extra phrase in their daily prayers; *"Ya hazir ya maujood fee kullil wujood"* which meant "O Ye

(Hazar Imam) who is apparent, O Ye who is present in all existence". Today, every Ismaili recites what was ordained for the Pakistani Jamat.

An Ismaili might say, agreed we had two Duas, but that is history; today, under the leadership of Aga Khan IV, we have a uniform code of religious practices and conduct, the world over. But the facts show, it is otherwise.

1. In Pakistan, under the auspices of Aga Khan's Institutions, Ismailis have been getting together to offer *Juma Namaz* (Friday afternoon Islamic congregational Prayers) for the last couple of decades. Juma Namaz for Ismailis, outside of Pakistan, however, is unheard of. Many Ismailis may be surprised to learn of this for the first time.

2. In Pakistan, many Jamatkhanas – old and new – have facilities for *Wadu* (ablution) like in Islamic Mosques. The newly built prestigious Jamatkhanas constructed at a cost of millions of dollars outside of Islamic States like Burnaby Jamat-khana in Canada (foundation laid 1982) and London Jamatkhana in England (foundation laid 1979), have no such facilities. They have toilets for men and women but no place to perform Wadu after the use of toilets.

3. In Pakistan, marriages of Ismaili couples are registered by the Jamati Officers after the couples have gone through the solemnity of 'Nikah' (an Islamic ritual for the marriage vows). In North America the marriages are registered without going through the 'Nikah' ceremony. A few Ismaili couples in Canada have of their own choice opted for 'Nikah'. Those couples have to find their own Mullah or a scholar who can per-

form the 'Nikah'. In most cases they have invited Sunni Imams from the Mosques, to perform the ceremony. A request for a uniform marriage custom for Ismailis was made, but so far it has not been responded.

An Ismaili begins his Dua with the popular seven verses of *Sura al-Fatihah*. Thereafter he recites a few phrases in Arabic which are ordained by Aga Khan. These phrases glorify Hazrat Ali and Hazar Imam, besides Allah. Thereafter he goes into prostration and sits up and recites the undermentioned "reconstituted and edited" verse, the text of which is reproduced photomechanically from an official book of Dua, transliterated and translated by The Ismailia Association for Pakistan, and published by The Shia Imami Ismailia Association for Africa, Mombasa, Kenya (1963).

Arabic text:

يَا أَيُّهَا الَّذِينَ آمَنُوا أَطِيعُوا اللهَ وَ أَطِيعُوا الرَّسُولَ
وَ أُوْلِي الْأَمْرِ مِنْكُمْ وَ كُلَّ شَىْءٍ أَحْصَيْنَاهُ فِي إِمَامٍ مُبِينٍ ۔

Transliterated text:

> Ya ayyuhal-lazeena amnoo, ati-Ullah wa ati-ur-Rasoola wa Ulil Amri minkum. Wa kulla shai'in ahsainahu fee Imamim-mubeen.

English translation:

> O ye, who believe! obey God and obey the Apostle and (obey) those who hold Authority from amongst you. And we have vested (the knowledge and authority) of everything in the manifest Imam.

Gujrati translation:

> અય ઈમાન લાવનારાઓ ! તાબેદારી કરો અહ્‌દ્રાહ્‌ની. તાબેદારી કરો રસુલની અને (તાબેદારી કરો) હુકમના ધણીની જે તમારામાંથી છે, અને અમોએ દરેક વસ્તુનો સમાવેશ જાહેર ઈમામમાં કરેલ છે.

– 69 –

The majority of Ismailis do not have the faintest notion that the verse under question is a combination of two "edited" verses from the Quran. The top portion of the text is the beginning of verse 59 of chapter 4 and the last line is the end portion from verse 12 of chapter 36, of the Quran. In the Ismaili Tariqah, recitation of this reconstituted verse in the daily Dua is made obligatory, and, unlike in the Namaz, it cannot be substituted with any other verse or verses from the Quran. Anyone who has not read the original text of the Quran in Arabic or its transliteration, would not be able to detect the editing, because the coupling of the two partial verses is done in such a professional manner that the enjoining fragment begins with the word "wa" in Arabic, meaning "and". In the Gujrati translation, verse 59 ends with a comma (,) instead of a period (.), and then continues further with the portion from verse 12, making the two separate verses into one.

Motives behind editing of verses

To pinpoint the motives, one has to divide the "reconstituted verse" into two sections (A & B) and then study them individually. The translation of section A of the reconstituted verse reads:

> "O ye, who believe! obey God and obey the Apostle and (obey) those who hold Authority from amongst you".

The **entire verse** 4/59 reads as below:

> "O ye, who believe! obey Allah and obey the messenger, and those who hold authority from amongst you; **and if ye have a dispute concerning any matter refer it to Allah and the messenger if ye are**

believers in Allah and the Last Day. That is better and more seemly in the end".

Reading the entire text, it is quite simple and easy to see what was expunged and why. The object was to hide that part of the Original Message that could open a door for Ismailis to step forward and question the decisions taken by "those who hold authority from among you" (*Ulil amr minkum*). The obedience to Aga Khan, the "*Ulil amr minkum*", would no longer remain unequivocal and unopposed.

Imam's decision can be disputed – The Quran

The deleted portion clearly indicates that a believer can be at variance with his "*Ulil amr minkum*" (Imam) and can dispute Imam's judgement. Furthermore, in the event that a dispute is raised, concerning any matter, then the Quranic Laws will overrule the Commands of an Imam by virtue of the proviso stipulated in the omitted portion of the Supreme Command of Allah. If an Ismaili is a believer in Allah and the Day of Judgement, then obeying the Quranic Laws is the right course, whether the "*Ulil amr minkum*" likes it or not. Farmans of an Imam can be disputed, but not the Commands of Allah.

> "None can dispute concerning the Revelations of Allah save those who disbelieve, so let not their turn of fortune in the land deceive thee".
>
> *Holy Quran 40/4*

To establish the motive behind the editing of the section B, the end portion of the reconstituted verse, one has to compare the translation of the fragmented portion, as it appears in the book of Dua, with the entire verse as it appears in the Quran.

The well known translator Abdullah Yusuf Ali's translation of verse 36/12 is:

> "Verily We shall give life to the dead, and *We record* (*naktubu*) that which they send before and that which they leave behind, and of all things have We taken account in a clear book".

Translator M.M. Pickthall's translation reads:

> "Lo! We it is who bring the dead to life. **We record** that which they send before (them), and their footprints. And all things We have kept in a clear register".

Below is the translation of the fragmented verse as it appears in the book of Dua, published by the Ismailia Association for Africa, Mombasa. Please note that the preceding three lines from the original verse have been intentionally expunged by the one who created this Unique Dua for Ismailis. As mentioned before, the Dua was authorized and given to his followers by Aga Khan III.

> "And we have vested (the knowledge and authority) of everything in the manifest Imam."

There is no explanation given as to why or from where the words "the knowledge and authority" within the brackets, have been inserted. Ismailis who memorize the above translation, always quote it inclusive of the words within the brackets, as if these words were part of the Revelation. Even the missionaries who preach the subject of Imamat say that Allah has vested the knowledge and authority of everything in Mawlana Hazar Imam – the Aga Khan.

In line with all other Ismaili authors of the past and present, Al-Waiz Abualy has over and over again quoted the above mentioned *last line* of verse 36/12 in his book. Ismaili authors do not publish the verse 36/12 in full, although it is only a small verse of just four lines. The reason is obvious. Whichever way they switch the words and tamper with their translation, under no circumstances would they be able to make the translation of the first three lines of the text so as to connect it with the **distorted** translation of the fourth line. Attribution of the word *"Imamim-mubeen"* to a living person makes it totally impossible for the translator to translate the word *"naktubu"* of the second line. The word *"naktubu"* means **"we write"** or **"we record"**. How can a translator justify the act of "writing" to be an act of "vesting in a living person and his successors"?

On the other hand, it is very simple for the translators like Yusuf Ali or Pickthall to justify their translations of *"Imamim-mubeen"* as "clear book" or "clear register" because in verse 46/12 Allah has called the *"Kitabu Musa"* (Book of Moses) – *"Imaaman"*.

Double Prostrations

Some Ismailis would say the Aga Khan is God, period. They would attribute 100% divinity to their Imam *(nauzbillah)*. Some would observe the age old practice of *"Taqiyya"*, meaning, permissible dissimulation; believe one thing with your heart but say another with your mouth in public. Most of the Ismailis are so confused that they avoid discussing the subject in order to escape embarrassment. There are some Ismailis who openly deny the Aga Khan's divinity. Ismaili scholars and missionaries are also divided on the issue. As we will see ahead, their Imam has created more confusion than clarification on the fundamental issue of divinity.   That not withstanding, **all these Ismailis**, wherever in the world they may be living, go to their Jamatkhanas and recite the same Dua. In the Dua they prostrate and recite:

> *"Allahumma laka sujoodi wa ta 'ati"* meaning "**O Allah**, to Thee is my prostration and obedience".

Immediately after the last prostration of the Dua, they **all** join in the supplementary Dua called *"Tasbih"*. At the end of the *"Tasbih"* they go into physical prostration, touch their foreheads to the floor, and recite:

> "Accept our humble beseechings of Tasbihs (for forgiveness of sins, pleadings for prosperity, pleas for health and wealth, petitions for easing problems, etc, etc) in Your presence, *Mawlana* (Our Lord), *Shah* (King), *Karim al-Hussaiyni* (Karim Aga Khan), *Hazar* (Present) *Imam.*"

What a Unique Prayer and Unique Supplementary Prayer. Double Prayers and Double Prostrations. One to Allah, the other to Aga Khan.

Aga Khan has yet to disclaim Divinity

Whenever an article (e.g. LIFE, International – December, 1983) or an author (e.g. Mihir Bose in *'The Aga Khans'*) labels the Aga Khan as a "Living God", he reacts and vehemently denies, through his lawyers and secretariat, any claim of divinity either by himself or his grandfather. Yet, neither he nor his grandfather has ever told their followers to stop attributing divinity to them, or to stop seeking forgiveness from them for sins, or to stop prostrating in the Imam's name or to **stop reciting Ginans which openly attribute Total Divinity to him** - in spite of appeals and requests by both, Ismailis and non-Ismailis, that this be done.

If Karim Aga Khan had taken a firm and consistent stand either way on the issue of divinity, and also acted accordingly within, as well as outside of the community, then the Ismaili Tariqah would no longer be called a Unique Tariqah. It would either be an *"Islamic Tariqah"* in its true sense or a totally *"Non-Islamic Tariqah"*.

In Karachi, Pakistan I had paid a sum of rupees fifty one into the treasury of Aga Khan and taken my turn standing in a long queue for a special *"Chhata"* (forgiving sins by sprinkling holy water), by Karim Aga Khan. One by one, each Ismaili who had paid the pre-scribed amount for *"Mahdan ka Chhata"* (Day of Judge-ment's Chhata) and was of over the age of 45 years, ap-proached the Aga Khan. He sprinkled holy water on the face of each and said: *"I have forgiven your sins"*. On the Day of Judgment, we would not be questioned about the forgiven sins. Before forgiving my sins, he did not ques-tion me what my sins were, as if he knew everything. He spoke in my ear and said that *all* my sins were forgiven. Does it not require divinity to forgive *all* sins?

". . .And who can forgive sins except Allah?"
Holy Quran 3 / 135

Before that, in Bombay and Poona, India, his grand-father, Aga Khan III had sprinkled water on my face and forgiven my sins on many, many occasions. These ceremonies of *"Chhatta for the Day of Judgement"* have been performed, even after the denial of Divinity in the High Courts of London in 1986.

Now the question is: Can these Ismailis turn around and question the authority of Karim Aga Khan and his grandfather for forgiving the sins or *all* sins, since he has publicly denied that either had Divinity? Can they ask for financial and spiritual restitutions?

After studying the past as well as the present performances of the Jamat, even an Ismaili has to admit the fact that the Imam's authority has at all times prevailed over and superseded the Quranic commands. The Constitution of the Shia Imami Ismaili Muslims defines the authority of the *"Farmans of Mawlana Hazar Imam"*. It goes so far as to say that his Farmans shall prevail over the Constitution, and that a later Farman shall prevail over an earlier. In other words, the Constitution can be scrapped and disposed of by Mawlana Hazar Imam at any time and place by a single Farman. No explanation is needed. No justification is demanded. The Constitution is silent, however, regarding the "Farman of Allah" – the Quran.

> "Not one of the beings in the heavens and the earth but must come to (Allah) most Gracious **as a servant**."
>
> *Holy Quran 19/93*

> "Unto Him is the real prayer. Those unto whom they pray beside Allah respond to them not at all, save as one who stretcheth forth his hands towards water (asking) that it may come unto his mouth, and it will never reach it. The prayer of disbelievers goeth astray".
>
> *Holy Quran 13/14*

10

Unique Segregation

"Dasond" – an inflated "Zakat"

This summer, I had the pleasure of meeting an influential Ismaili social worker, who had just returned from his tour of India and Pakistan. He had one very important and valid question on his mind. Since I have lived in Pakistan, he imagined that I would be in a better position to answer his query or else elucidate on the subject. His question was in connection with the Aga Khan Hospital in Karachi, Pakistan.

One of the senior administrators of the Aga Khan Hospital, who keeps on visiting continent after continent, collecting millions of dollars for the hospital project had informed the Jamat that in Pakistan, "Muslims" (a term used by Ismaili Muslims for non-Ismailis) are funnelling their 'Zakat' (poor dues) contributions to the hospital.

Medical services offered to the needy and money spent in that cause is considered as *"Zakat"* contributed, by the Muslims of Pakistan.

The question of the visitor was that if that was the case, then can he adjust his past donations to the Aga Khan Hospital against his future contributions of *"Dasond"* (an Ismaili term for Zakat)? Alternatively, can he funnel his Dasond money to the Aga Khan Hospital, in the future, or to any other Ismaili *"Boardings"* (term used for Orphanages)? He also mentioned that back home it was not difficult to collect cash under the table. In Canada, paying of the Dasond in cash to *Mukhi* (Minister of the Aga Khan), without obtaining a receipt, poses accounting problems. The amount contributed cannot be deducted as expenses on his income tax returns. Physical cash has to be withdrawn from a bank and handed over personally to the Ministers of the Aga Khan, in the Jamatkhanas, every month. At times, there are long queues at the banks and also in the Jamatkhanas to submit the Dasond money. Finally, there is a question of savings. Contributions paid to a registered institution having a tax exemption means a big saving in the income-tax.

My response was that the senior administrator he had named was not only a roving ambassador but a very highly paid kingpin at the Aga Khan Hospital. I had no reason to doubt the statement made by him in public or before the Jamat. If *"Muslims"* can regard their donations to the Hospital as Zakat, then Ismailis can offset their donations to the Hospital as Dasond – which is an inflated Zakat. To be precise, the word "Dasond" is a derivation from *"Das-ans"* or *"Das-ant"*, which means

"Tenth part". A Zakat of "Ten percent" means Dasond. To this Zakat is added 2 1/2% share of the 'Pir'. Hence, the present Aga Khan, who is an Imam as well as a Pir, collects Zakat and Khums which comes to 12 1/2%. Under the circumstances, in my personal opinion, an Ismaili can pay 2 1/2% to Aga Khan as his share of 'Pir' and the balance of 10% can be offset against his contributions as "poor-dues", to charitable hospitals and orphanages, if he so chooses.

Note: Under the normal circumstances, a Muslim pays only 2 1/2% of his personal assets after all expenses, as Zakat once a year. Whereas, an Ismaili pays 12 1/2% or 25%, as the case may be, of his gross income to Karim Aga Khan, as Dasond, every month. What Aga Khan does with that money or what he is supposed to do is unknown; nor is an Ismaili expected to know.

Discriminations and Segregations

Every Ismaili is supposed to pay 12 1/2% of his **gross** income as Dasond. There are thousands of Ismailis in Canada who pay 25% of their gross income to Aga Khan. They are members of an exclusive *"Mandli"* (group) called 'Mubarak Mandli' or 'One-fourth Mandli'. They hold secret monthly meetings called *"One-fourth Majlis"* in Jamatkhanas throughout the world. They pay their Dasond of 25% in their Majlis to the Mukhis of their Mandlis and not to the Jamati Mukhis. An Ismaili who is not a member of 'Mubarak Mandli' cannot participate in their Majlises. Aga Khan gives them private audiences and makes special Farmans. He also gives them special blessings. My wife was a member of a Mubarak Mandli. She paid 25% of her personal income, or pocket money received from me and also on the gifts and prizes received by her. My wife would not tell me the Farmans made for their 'Mubarak Mandlis'. She had a book of 'Private and Confidential Farmans' for her group which I was not allowed to touch. I believe they consider Aga Khan as their **"Partner"** or vice versa. I am told there is a group above the Mubarak. The members of these groups, I am told, pay 33 1/3% of their income to Aga Khan. I have not met any member of this Mandli because they would not reveal their identity, nor would anyone confirm their existence.

On the other hand, I was a member of *"Noorani Mandli"* and my wife was not a member. I was not allowed to tell my wife what transpired in our Majlises nor what was revealed by Aga Khan to our private group of elites. To become a member of "Noorani" I had to pay a considerable sum, to the treasurer of Aga Khan, as an entrance fee. I was not issued a receipt for the amount tendered nor a membership card or a certificate. When I attended the first Majlis of my Noorani Mandli, I was surprised to see that practically every well-to-do Ismaili was in the group. Non-members – usually those who could not afford the entrance fees – were not allowed to participate in our Majlises. After the Majlis they were invited to help as volunteers, to serve our lunches and dinners. Virtually an Ismaili is being segregated from another Ismaili or a husband segregated from his wife and vice versa.

Before joining the 'Noorani' I passed through half a dozen smaller segregated groups or Mandlis; each having their own designated place in the community. After my joining the Noorani Mandli, I was told of a few other Mandlis that were above my group. I have no idea where this hierarchy of elite and super elite Ismailis come to an end. All I know is that the higher the Mandli, the higher the entrance fee and the more segregated you become. Aga Khan gives separate audiences to each

Mandli and makes appropriate Farmans. The more you pay, the closer you are considered to be to Aga Khan.

His Farmans give you that sense of elevation. The names designated to these Mandlis also identify the class distinctions. Surprisingly, the only requisite for it is, how much you can afford to pay in "cash". There are Mandlis which are equivalent to clubs of the recipients of "Purple Heart" or "Victoria Cross". The Membership criteria – money. In other words, money is the root of all elevations and distinctions.

Triple Taxation

From my personal experience I can say that an Ismaili bread-earner would pay 12 1/2% of his income to Aga Khan. He then would give his wife pocket money to buy her clothing and other needs. Then his wife would pay 25% of the pocket money, as her Mubarak Mandli dues to Aga Khan. Then, she would give her children a weekly allowance. Each child would pay 12 1/2% to Aga Khan out of his or her allowance.

I have often asked missionaries, "Why the wife should pay 25%, if the husband has already paid 12 1/2% prior to the payment of pocket money?" Since I was not a member of the Mubarak, it was not an appropriate subject for me to discuss, and missionaries are not allowed to discuss matters pertaining to "Mubarak" with non-members.

A childhood friend of mine is a member of "Mubarak" and so is his wife. In their family, the rate of "triple Dasond" is 25% – 25% and 12 1/2%. That gives me some consolation that in my family the rate was 12 1/2% – 25% and 12 1/2%.

During the period of his Imamat, Aga Khan III had made very strict Farmans for Dasond. Some of his Farmans suggested that losses may occur by fire and sickness if Dasond was not paid in full, and also mentioned that without the Dasond there was no foundation for the religion. An Ismaili cannot attain "Noorani Deedar" or make any progress in his esoteric meditation if he defaults in his payment of Dasond. On the other hand, contributors of Dasonds will be repaid here, and hereafter in the ratio of 1:125,000.

The present Aga Khan has not made any specific Farmans for Dasonds, but by the same token has not stopped collecting Dasond or has not stopped giving Mubarak members, special blessings.

An evening with Aga Khan

On the evening of February 8th 1970, Karim Aga Khan was sitting on a sofa in the Prayer Hall *(Jamatkhana)* of Muhammadi Girls' Academy, Karachi, with his shoes on.

I was standing beside him with my shoes off and nearly 200 resident boarders of the Academy and staff members were sitting on the floor, facing the Aga Khan. They all were reciting *'Salwat'* with their hands clasped and raised.

It is an age old Ismaili custom that whenever and wherever the Aga Khan pays a visit, to give his *'Deedar'* (glimpse) or *'Mulaqat'* (audience), the followers continuously recite 'Salwat' after 'Salwat'. This recitation starts from the moment he steps into the hall and it continues aloud until he settles down on his special chair or sofa. The recited 'Salwat' is in Arabic, which translates; "Peace of Allah be upon Muhammad and the progeny of Muhammad". Karim Aga Khan claims to be a progeny of Prophet Muhammad.

The great irony of this practice is that before the arrival of Aga Khan, an Ismaili missionary would deliver a sermon on the importance of having a 'Deedar' of Aga Khan. Besides other things he would invariably profess that Allah has manifested Himself or Allah's Noor has manifested itself in the body of Aga Khan. The *Zahir* (manifested) Imam is a *Mazhar* (literally, copy or manifest) of Allah. His Deedar is the Deedar of Allah. All sins of a *'Momin'* (true believer) are washed away with one glimpse *(Deedar)* of Aga Khan. Both the above concepts, namely; 'Noor of Allah manifested in a human body' and 'Mazhar of Allah' are but, modified versions of the 'Incarnations of God' *(Avtaras)* – a Hindu philosophy. Aga Khan is considered to be the tenth incarnation of 'Lord Vishnu' by Ismailis.

It may sound unrealistic, but the fact is that upon the arrival of the Aga Khan, the same missionary who has proclaimed Karim Aga Khan to be a *Mazhar* (copy); an *Avtara* (incarnation) and a *Noor* (light) of Allah, would lead the recitation of 'Salwat' from the same dais. Now, the followers who have come to get their sins washed by one glimpse of Aga Khan, are praying to "Allah" to send "Peace" upon the soul of Aga Khan, although his soul is a copy, incarnation and light of Allah Himself!!! *(nauzbillah)*

After the usual ceremonies of Niaz, Memanis, Blessings and Farmans, Karim Aga Khan was about to get up from his sofa when the innocent young girls of the Academy, who were dressed in white, began crying. Tears started rolling down their tiny cheeks. The girls were seeking forgiveness, but for what? Aga Khan was surprised. He asked me what was the problem. I asked Mukhiyani the reason. She began talking to Aga Khan in her usual manner and language, which Aga Khan could not understand. She was speaking about 'Dasond' and was pointing at her wrist. With a look of bewilderment, Karim Aga Khan – the one "who has the knowledge and authority of everything" – asked me to explain what the Mukhiyani had related.

"Dasond" from Charitable Donations

Before I continue further, I wish to inform you that the Ismailia Youth Services – a parent body of Muhammadi Girls' Academy and Prince Aly Boys' Academy – had hired an Ismaili lady-missionary to teach Ismailism to the girls of the Academy. She was a member of special Mandli mentioned before. She had probably indoctrinated the girls about 'Dasond' to be paid from the Charitable Donations collected. I clarified before Karim Aga Khan that the girls of the Academy who were crying, had certain concepts about 'Dasond'. Because the 12 1/2% Dasond was not being paid from donations collected, they felt that the food prepared from the money was not pure. Pointing to the veins on her hand the Mukhiyani tried to describe the fact that the blood produced from the food also was impure. Consequently, the girls could not progress in their *'Bandgi'* (meditation) between 4 and 5 (a.m.) every morning.

Thereupon, Aga Khan made a Farman to the girls which stated that any money received by him as Dasond is returned. If they paid the Dasond it will be paid back. This was not a simple Farman, to pay or not to pay the Dasond.

In the following meeting of the Ismailia Youth Services I was bombarded with questions. I was requested to strain my memory and repeat the Farman verbatim precisely, because it could be misinterpreted. Unfortunately, no other member of the Youth Services or of the Academy was present at that moment. I could not be precise as I did not make notes. During their two hour tour of boys' and girls' Academy, I must admit I answered dozens of questions and heard that many remarks, advises and jokes from their Highnesses.

The issue was delicate and concerned the fundamental aspects of Ismaili religion. The members could not come to a unanimous decision as to the paying of the Dasond, out of charity money. It was resolved that a guidance be sought from Aga Khan by writing a letter.

Aga Khan replied that the Ismaili Youth Services should pay a token amount, every month, in the Jamatkhana as a Dasond. Now came the real problem, how to pay the Dasond in cash without any written acknowledgement of the payment? The treasurer would not release funds every month without a voucher because the auditors would not pass such withdrawals. The second question was about justifying to the donars the payment of Dasond. Some of them were giving donations in lieu of the Dasond and they would not like their contributions channelled to the treasury of Aga Khan.

Finally, a member of the Youth Services agreed to pay the sum demanded by Aga Khan, in the Jamatkhana every month, for a period of one year out of her pocket. Before the year was over I was nominated as President of the Council and had to relinquish my post with the Ismailia Youth Service and Muhammadi Girls' Academy. I am not sure, but I believe that the Farman of the Aga Khan to pay Dasond, from the **charitable donations**, is still being diligently followed. The money continues to go from the pocket of the Youth Services or its members into the collection bag of the Mukhi Saheb.

Today, the girls of the Academy who were crying must be grown and perhaps, they may be wondering was it necessary to pay "poor dues" *(Dasond)* out of charity money? Was non payments a reason for not gaining progress in their 'Bandgi'? "Do we have to follow the teachings of our teachers, missionaries or parents, if they are teaching us or asking us to practice a belief that is sinful in the eyes of Allah?"

Allah says:

> "We have enjoined on man kindness to parents; but if they strive to make thee join with Me that of which thou hast no knowledge, then **obey them not**. Unto Me is your return and I shall tell you what ye used to do."
>
> *Holy Quran 29/8*

On the subject of early morning *"Bandgi"* (meditation) for acquiring spiritual elevation and discipline, Muslims who follow the Quranic guidances do practice it. In Islam, the midnight and after midnight contemplation and prayers are called *"Tahajjud"*. The Prophet also used to practice it.

> "Truly the rising by night is most potent for governing (the soul), and most suitable for (framing) the Word."
>
> *Holy Quran 73/6*

Note: For more information refer to verses 17/79 and 73/20 of the Holy Quran.

11

Unique History

Ismailism cannot exist without a Living Imam

There can be no Christianity without a Christ and his "Crucifixion."

There can be no Ismailism without a Living *(Hazar)* Imam and the "Proclamation" (made by the Prophet).

The "Hazar Imam" is not a legitimate Imam unless he is a bonafide, lawful, lineal (physical) descendant of the Prophet's son-in-law, Ali ibn Abi Talib, and Bibi Fatima (daughter of the Prophet).

A single break or flaw in this hereditary chain of

uninterrupted generations means that the Imamat "Proclaimed" by the Prophet, has come to an end. The religion that was founded upon "the Proclamation" cannot exist without a designated direct descendant of Ali. The genealogy of Ali is the life-line of Ismailism. The Ismaili Constitution specifies that succession to Imamat is by way of *'Nass'* (designation), **from amongst any of his male descendants** whether they be sons or remoter issue. The term "remoter issue" is derived from the 'Will' of Aga Khan III. The said Will also records: "(. . . that under Shia Moslem law the issue of a son is not an heir if there be a son alive)". However, Karim Aga Khan was appointed Imam when his father Aly Khan was alive.

I have often asked these questions to Ismailis. What is so unique or extraordinary about the Ismaili Tariqah? What makes you so confident that you are on *Siratul Mustaqim* (the straight path), and that others are not? The usual answer that I have received is , "Look at the preservation and safekeeping of this uninterrupted chain of physical descendants of Ali, generation after generation, for the last 1400 years. Show us another similar hereditary line. If Karim Aga Khan was not a divinely designated "Guide" (*Imam*) to lead the *Ummah* (Universal Muslim Brotherhood), the link would have been cut off long ago, alike those of Musa Kazim, Imam of the Ithna'ashris and that of Musta'ali, Imam of the Bohras." The answer is proud, assertive and defiant. Author Abualy's statement on the issue is even more challenging. On page 53, he writes:

> "CONSIDER: A lie does not last long. If the Ismaili Imams were not the True Imams their lie would have lasted for a generation or two but not for all these fourteen hundred years and fifty generations without interruption. The 'Imams' of a few offshoots of

this Holy Line of Imamat had, in the past, claimed Imamat wrongly but disappeared within a short time. Their 'Imamat' did not last for more than five generations."

Ismaili Tariqah

The argument may sound logical because Ismailis are now talking of physical evidence from the pages of history. But the question is how do Ismailis know that these 50 generations are **without interruption**?

From his childhood, an Ismaili is commanded by his Imam to recite in his Dua, three times in a day, the entire genealogy of his Hazar Imam, from Ali to Aga Khan. Furthermore, he has been listening to lectures and sermons of his religious school teachers and missionaries that the sacred chain of 50 generations – a physical link from father to son – is an uninterrupted hereditary link. Ismaili missionaries have been narrating historical events and miracles recorded in a book of history of Ismaili Imams, called *'Noorum-Mubin'* (Manifest Light). The word *'Noorum-Mubin'* has been interpreted by its publisher as *"The Sacred Cord of God"* and described as "A Glorious History of Ismaili Imams'. This book of history is written in Gujrati and was first published in 1936 in Bombay. I have asked Ismaili missionaries if they have ever compared the data of "Noorum-Mubin" with other non-Ismaili sources. Their familiar answer has been that they are theologians and not students of history. Author Abualy, a missionary, explains the reason for his writing "A Brief History of Ismailism." In the preface he writes:

> "It is difficult for an average person, particularly the Ismaili youth, to read voluminous Noorum-Mubin in Gujrati or Urdu to know about the history of Ismailism."

If that be the case, then imagine, how difficult it would be for an average Ismaili youth to compare the history of his Imams with other non-Ismaili sources. Besides, this voluminous 'Noorum-Mubin' has been out of print for the last 25 years. The Sacred Chain of designated Imams, from father to son, is the principal reason and underlying root of Hazar Imam's authority to **"lead"** Ismailis. Hazar Imam is the nucleus of Ismailism. The book of history of Ismaili Imams – 'Noorum-Mubin,' – which can provide the physical evidence to support his hereditary claim to "lead" as a Supreme Authority is not available at any price. Under the chairmanship of Mowlana Hazar Imam it was resolved:

> "The Nooran Mubeen no longer to be made available to the Jamat as a standard textbook of Ismaili history."

Paris Conference Resolution No. 3.3.1 – 1975

Is the "Sacred Chain" of 50 Generations Uninterrupted?

Below is a chart of 50 generations of Hazrat Ali (son-in-law and cousin of the Prophet). The names of 49, so-called designated descendants of Ali, are copied from a book of Ismaili Dua published by the Ismaili Association for Africa – 1963. The three Ismaili sources compared are:

1. 'A Brief History of Ismailism' (English) written by Abualy A. Aziz and published in 1985 (3rd Edition), from Toronto, Canada. The book has been recommended by the Ismailia Association in **Africa**.

2. 'A concise text of History of Ismaili Imams' (Gujrati) published in 1980 (3rd revised edition), by H.R.H. The Aga Khan Ismailia Association for **Pakistan**.

3. *"Noorum-Mubin, A Glorious History of Ismaili Imams"* (Gujrati) published in 1951 (3rd revised edition), by the Ismailia Association for **India**.

In the comparative chart printed below, under columns number 2 and 3, the years of births are only mentioned when they differ from those mentioned under column 1.

Genealogy of Ismaili Imams

No.	Name of Imam	Year of Birth		
		Recorded by Abualy (1)	Recorded by Pakistan (2)	Recorded by India (3)
1	Moulana Aly	600		
2	Husayn	626		
3	Zainil-abedeen	659		
4	Muhammad al-Baqir	677		
5	J'afar as Sadiq	702	699	

Ismailis & Ithna'asharis separated from here.

6	Ismail	719	unknown	unknown

Controversies exist about the place & year of his death.

7	Muhammad bin Ismail	746	740	750
8	Wafi Ahmad	766	unknown	unknown
9	Taqi Muhammad	790	unknown	unknown
10	Raziyuddin Abdullah	825	unknown	unknown

Year of death differs between Ismaili sources by 6 years.

11	Muhammad al-Mahdi	859	873	873

Year of birth differs by 14 years. Start of Fatimid Dynasty in Africa. Qarmatians secedes from Ismailis.

		(1)	(2)	(3)
12	al-Qaim	893		
13	al-Mansoor	913	914	
14	al-Muiz	930	931	931
15	al-Aziz	953	955	
16	al-Hakim bi amrillah	986	985	

Year of death uncertain 1018 or 1021 or 1034!

		(1)	(2)	(3)
17	az-Zahir	1005		
18	al-Mustansir-billah	1029		

Ismailis & Bohras separated from here after.

		(1)	(2)	(3)
19	Nizar	1045		

Ismailis are also called Nizari Ismailis because they recognized Nizar as their Imam.

		(1)	(2)	(3)
20	Hadi	1069	unknown	unknown
21	Muhtadi	unknown	unknown	unknown
22	Qahir	1121	unknown	unknown
23	Ala-Zikrihis-Salam	1152	1126/27	1114

Year of birth differs. As per source 1 he died at the age of 14 years; as per source 2 at the age of 40 years; and as per source 3 at the age of 52 years.

		(1)	(2)	(3)
24	A'la Muhammad	1155	1147	unknown

According to source No. 1 he was born when his father was 3 years old!

		(1)	(2)	(3)
25	Jalaluddin Hasan	1186	1166/1167	unknown

Year of birth differs by about 20 years.

		(1)	(2)	(3)
26	Ala-uddin Muhammad	about 1211	1213	1213
27	Ruknuddin Khair Shah	1228	1230	unknown

Last Imam of Alamut. "Period of hiding" for Imams starts.

		(1)	(2)	(3)
28	Shamsuddin Muhammad	1250	unknown	unknown

		(1)	(2)	(3)
29	Qasim Shah	unknown	unknown	unknown
30	Islam Shah	unknown	unknown	unknown
31	Muhammad bin Islam Shah	unknown	unknown	unknown
32	Mustansir-billah	unknown	unknown	unknown
33	Abdus-salam	1456	unknown	unknown
34	Ghareeb Meerza	unknown	unknown	unknown
35	Abuzar Ali	unknown	unknown	unknown
36	Murad Meerza	unknown	unknown	unknown
37	Zulfiqar Ali	unknown	unknown	unknown
38	Nooruddin Ali	1513	unknown	unknown
39	Khalilullah Ali	unknown	unknown	unknown

From #33 to 38 = 5 generations, within 57 years!

		(1)	(2)	(3)
40	Nizar	unknown	unknown	unknown
41	Sayyed Ali	unknown	unknown	unknown
42	Hasan Ali	unknown	unknown	unknown
43	Qasim Ali	1675	unknown	unknown
44	Abul-Hasan Ali	unknown	unknown	unknown
45	Khalilullah Ali	1749	unknown	
46	Hasan Ali	1805	1804	1804

Year of death differs by 1 year.

		(1)		
47	Ali Shah	1830		
48	Sultan Muhammad Shah	1877		

	(1)	(2)	(3)
—	(Aly Soloman Khan)	13/06/1911	13/06/1910

He was declared 'Heir Apparent' by the 48th Imam in 1930.
But in the final Will, his son Karim was declared the 49th Imam.

49	Karim al-Husayni	1936

Place of birth uncertain. Could be Paris or Geneva.

A careful study of the above chart indicates that the physical evidence in support of the preservation of Divine Cord (hereditary link) is not so convincing. This is an introduction to the genealogy, the detailed account of the controversies is to follow. If one was to note all the conflicts between the Ismaili and non-Ismaili sources, it would fill many volumes. I have selected only a few controversies, where the evidence immediately casts serious doubts on the "historical facts".

Imam Ismail - the 6th Generation:

Controversy No. 1:

Non-Ismaili sources claim that the elder son Ismail was chosen as a successor by his father, but he died before his father. His younger brother Musa Kazim was chosen as the next successor. The majority of Shias, accept this to be the truth. They are called Shia Ithna'ashris.

Ismailis, the minority group of the Shia sect, refute the above. They claim that Ismail was secretly sent out by his father to Syria to protect him from his enemies, and that Ismail continued his Imamat from there and died in Salamiya, a town in Syria.

Note: The name "Ismaili" derives from this split in the Shia history.

Controversy No. 2:   **Where was Ismail buried?**

The non-Ismaili sources claim that the funeral of Ismail was taken out by his father and **his body is buried in Medina.** There are registered documents indicating his death and burial in Medina. Ismaili sources claim the funeral and the burial did take place in Medina, but it was a mock funeral, staged by his father to mislead the enemies.

Ismailis who have visited the city of Medina have informed me that they have recited *'Fateha'* on the grave of Ismail. The question is, why do Ismailis recite *'Fateha'* on the grave of Ismail which is in Medina, if his body was buried in Syria? How could it be possible that a notable Muslim leader of his time, Imam Jafar as Sadiq, have a public funeral of his grown son, go through the funeral services and the Islamic burial ceremonies, in front of the Muslims of the city without a body? And that too happened in the city of Medina – a centre of the Islamic Empire of his time!

Controversy No. 3:

On page 44, of *'A Brief History of Ismailism'*, Abualy quotes:

"The whole **crux of Ismail's claim** to Imamat lay in his being alive at the time of his father's death; and this has been proved from various references by his contemporaries and historians of a later period, from which it can be discovered that Ismail **died twenty years after his father.** (References: *Tarikhe Jahangusha; Tarikhe Farishta and Umdat-ul-Talib)*"

On page 41, Abualy records that the father of Ismail died in Medina, in August, 765 A.D.

If Ismail died **20 years** after his father, that makes 765+20 = **785 A.D.** as the year of death of Ismail.

On page 47, Abualy quotes, Ismail died in **775 A.D.**

Abualy has thus nullified the "crux" cited by recording Ismail's death in 775 and not in 785 A.D.

Controversy No. 4:

On page 44, Abualy writes:

> "Bernard Lewis refers to *'Dastur al Munajjimin'* according to which Ismail was the first hidden Imam. His concealment began in 145 A.H. (762 A.D.) but his death did not occur till **seven years later.**"

The equivalent year for 145 A.H. has been inserted by me within the brackets, which is 762 A.D.

If Ismail died "7 years later", then his year of death should be 762+7 = **769A.D.**

On page 47, Abualy quotes, Ismail died in **775 A.D.** (Not 769 A.D.)

Here again Abualy has invalidated facts quoted by him.

Controversy No. 5:

Abualy has recorded as below:

On page 42; Ismail was born in 719 A.D.

On page 41; Ismail succeeded his father (became Imam) at the age of 48 years.

On page 47; Ismail died after 10 years of Imamat.

Adding the above three we get $719+48+10 = $ **777 A.D.** as the year of Ismail's death.

Conclusion:

From the above mentioned data, we have the following:

a) As per Controversy No. 3 Ismail died in 785

b) As per Controversy No. 4 Ismail died in 769

c) As per Controversy No. 5 Ismail died in 777

d) Abualy records on page 47 Ismail died in 775

Non-Ismaili sources claim Ismail died before his father, who died in 765 A.D.

Imam Muhammad, the 7th Generation:

Controversy No.1:

Non-Ismaili sources claim that Ismail died during the lifetime of his father, without ascending to the throne of Imamat. Therefore, Ismail's son, Muhammad's claim of having succeeded as the next Imam is invalid.

All the above mentioned Ismaili sources claim that Ismail's son Muhammad succeeded his father as the next Imam, in **775 A.D.**

Controversy No. 2:   ***Ismaili sources contradict each other.***

How old was Imam Muhammad when he succeeded his father in 775 A.D.?

a) On page 77, 'Noorum-Mubin' records he was **26** years old.

b) On page 48, Abualy records he was **29** years old. (Born in 746 A.D.)

c) On page 44, Ismailia Association for Pakistan records he was **35** years old.

Imam Raziyuddin Abdullah, the 10th Generation:

Controversy No. 1:

The following is a totally outlandish record.

On page 51, Abualy writes and I quote:

> "Once in the year **266 A.H. (A.D. 880)**, he (Raziyuddin) was travelling to Najaf. He met Ibn Haushab..."

On the next page Abualy writes:

> "...he (Raziyuddin) fell sick and died on Sunday the first of Rajab, **262 A.H. (A.D. 876)**..."

Note: Imam died in 876 A.D. but he met someone **four years after his death.**

Incredible as it may sound, this book of history has been in circulation since 1947, as a text book for high school students in religious classes. This edition was published in Canada in 1985 and yet strangely enough this data remains unrectified!

Imam Muhammad al-Mahdi, the 11th Generation:

Controversy No. 1:   ***Two Mahdi or one?***

    a)   Abualy writes on page 53, "Mowlana Imam Mohammed al-Mehdi was born on Sunday, the fifteenth of Ramzan, 245 A.H. (October, 859)..."

    b)   Ismailia Associations for Pakistan, as well as for India, record that Mahdi was born on Monday, the twelfth of Sawwal, 260 A.H. (31 July, 873).

Both are Ismaili sources. Both are precise as to the Day, Date, Month and Year, yet they differ by nearly 14 years.

Controversy No. 2:

    a)   Abualy writes, al-Mahdi was born in Mahmoudabad, a town near Rey in Iran.

    b)   Ismailia Associations for Pakistan and India record that he was born in the city of Askar Mukarram in Syria.

Controversy No. 3:

    a)   On page 52, Abualy records that the father of Mahdi died in Constantinople, Turkey in 876.

    b)   Ismailia Associations for Pakistan and India record that the father of Mahdi died in Askar Mukarram, Syria in 882.

Note: The above mentioned controversies give us two sets of:—

    a)   Dates of birth.

b)   Places of birth.

c)   Dates of Father's death.

d)   Places of Father's death.

How can one individual have such a dual record? Were there two individuals, both known as Muhammad al-Mahdi? The answer can be found in the next controversy.

Controversy No. 4:

Noorum-Mubin records on page 98 that Ismailis had lost contact with their Imam. Six leading missionaries gathered together in Askar Mukarram and declared:

> "We have lost the physical contact of our Imam. Our *Namaz* and *Fastings* have no meaning without an Imam. We do not know to whom to send the *Zakat* money. Therefore we must embark upon a mission of finding Imam".

They held a meeting of the leading Ismailis, collected donations, and resolved that the missionaries should travel in pairs, disguised as traders, from village to village in Persia, Iraq, Yemen and other countries. Noorum-Mubin has given a detailed account of their travel, names of these six missionaries and their methods of finding the Imam. The person they were looking for as their Imam had to meet the physical description as well as certain qualities they were asked to look for. After travelling through many countries missionary Abu Gafir and missionary Ziyad, who were travelling together, found a person that possessed the qualities they were looking for and matched the description. He was living in a remote *'Ashram'* (a monastic establishment) on a hilltop. Noorum-Mubin has recorded the name of this person as Abul Kassim Muhammed Abdullah son of Hussain son of Ahmed son of Abdullah. He became al-Mahdi.

On page 93, Noorum-Mubin has recorded a Prophecy made by Imam Razi Abdullah, and a doubtful *Hadith* (reported sayings of the Prophet) which says: **"300 years after me the Sun will rise from the West"**. This Prophecy, according to the Imam Razi Abdullah, was for the manifestation of *"Mahdi"* (a promised Messiah). This so called *Hadith* has been repeated once again on page 103 and Noorum Mubin has added an equally undependable *Riwayat* (legend) which goes on to say that the Prophet said; the name of the *"Mahdi"* to come 300 years after me, will be the same as mine (i.e.. Muhammad) and his father's name will also be the same as my father's name (i.e.. Abdullah).

The Ismaili missionaries were obviously aware of the Prophecy made by their Imam. The name of the person they discovered, and the name of his father, matched perfectly with the *Riwayat* attached to the so called *Hadith*, concerning the manifestation of "Mahdi". The prophesized period of 300 years and West of Arabia, also matched when this Abul Kassim Muhammed conquered the West (North West Africa). He was therefore called Ubayadullah Mahdi or Mohammad Mahdi, the prophesized deliverer or Messiah of Ismailis. The seat of Imamat moved from Syria to Africa. He became the first Imam of the Fatimid Dynasty in Egypt. Ismailis often refer to this period of Imamat in Egypt as the Golden Era of their "Fatimid Caliphate". Historians have called it the "anti- Caliphate of Cairo" (see 'Scandal' - Essays in Islamic Heresy - 1988, page 36).

On page 108, Noorum Mubin records that the Abbasid Caliphate had been accusing Ismailis that their Imam

Mahdi was not a descendant of Imam Ismail (the 7th Imam). He was a descendant of Abdullah Maimoon Al'kdah or son of Abdullah bin Sham Nusheri.

Note: Ismaili historians have recorded **two sets of records**. Are they positive as to which is the genuine record? Is one set for a **Son of Imam Raziyuddin**, with whom Ismailis had lost contact according to Noorum Mubin and, the other set for the discovered Mahdi, who is being recognized as a **successor to Imam Raziyuddin**?

The following controversies support the theory of **'Two Individuals'**.

Controversy No. 5:

Ismaili sources have not only maintained two sets of records, but have also given **dual names** to their Imams, as shown below —

11th Imam Muhammad Mahdi *alias* Abul Kassim

10th Imam Raziyuddin Abdullah *alias* Hussain

9th Imam Taqi Muhammad *alias* Ahmed

Controversy No. 6:

On page 97, Noorum Mubin has recorded that Qarmatians were followers of Imam Ismail bin Jafar as Sadiq. During 278 A.H. (the period of Imam Mahdi's Imamat), they rebelled against the mainstream of Syrian Ismailis (who had declared Abul Kassim as "Mahdi" and their Imam). Qarmatians appointed their own leader and seceded from the Imamat of Imam Mahdi. This group which had separated as Qarmatians concentrated in Iraq.

Note:

1. In Islamic history, Qarmatians are well known as notorious sub-sect of Ismailis who invaded Mecca and removed the Sacred Black Stone from *'Kabah'*. After 22 years of effort the Sacred Stone was finally recovered from them, upon payment of ransom money.

2. Imam Mahdi abolished the *Hajj* (pilgrimage to 'Kabah'). The reason is obvious after having read the above. This tradition still exists. *'Deedar'* (glimpse of Imam), is Ismaili's Hajj.

3. If Imam Mahdi had been a physical descendant of Ismail, then the Qarmatians would not have rebelled against him. They were staunch followers of Imam Ismail and his son and grandsons as far as Raziyud-din Abdullah.

Controversy No. 7:

Noorum Mubin is filled with hundreds of Miracles, scores of Riwayats, and Prophecies to support their historical data. The Ismailia Association for Pakistan was asked by Aga Khan IV to delete all such theological references in their concise text. To prove the Imamat of Mahdi, they have retained one prophecy and a miracle associated with it.

The Ismailia Association for Pakistan records:

> "One day Mahdi was taking a walk in a garden. He came upon a stream that had dried up since long ago. Mahdi kicked the ground and water started flowing in the stream. The gardener shouted: 'Imam Mahdi has **manifested**. Imam Mahdi has **manifested**'." Continuing the narration, Noorum

Mubin writes: "The gardener said to Imam Mahdi: 'My ancestors used to say; when Imam Mahdi will come, this stream will flow again. You are **indeed** our Imam Mahdi, because the water has started flowing in the stream'." (page 58)

Note: According to the Ismaili tradition, a designated son of the previous Imam, instantaneously becomes the next Imam, after the death of his father. If "Mahdi" was such a designated son, then the gardener and everyone in the city should have already known him as Imam Mahdi. Why did he have to shout "Imam Mahdi has **manifested**"?

Imam Hadi, the 20th Generation:

Controversy No.1:

Ismaili sources claim that Imam Mustansir-billah had designated his eldest son Nizar as the next Imam. But a younger son, al-Musta'ali, was scheming to depose his elder brother. When Mustansir-billah died, Musta'ali declared himself as Imam with the help of Prime Minister Afzal Badr Jamali. Imam Nizar and his two sons Ma'add and Hadi were imprisoned in Alexandria, Egypt. Those who accepted the Imamat of Musta'ali became Bohras or Mustalians. Those who accepted Nizar as their Imam became Nizari Ismailis (followers of Aga Khan).

Ismaili sources claim Hadi escaped from the prison and settled in the fort of Lamasar, Iran. The factual details of his escapement and the year of his escape are not available. Hadi married an Iranian lady and had a son named Muhtadi. The year of his marriage, and the year of the birth of his son are not known to Ismaili sources.

Non-Ismaili sources claim Hadi died in the prison of Alexandria without leaving a survivor. The Fatimid Dynasty came to an end for Nizari Ismailis, but it continued for Mustalians – the Bohras.

Imam Qahir, the 22nd Generation:

Controversy No. 1:

Ismaili sources claim that al-Qahir was the name of the 22nd Imam. He was son of Muhtadi and **father of Hasan**. Ismailia Associations for India and Pakistan have no record of the year of his birth.

Non-Ismaili sources claim 'Qahir Shah' or 'al-Qahir' is a title. Professor W.Ivanow writes:

> "Many believed that the title mentioned above, al-Qahir bi-amrillah, was **assumed by Hasan himself**"
>
> *Alamut and Lamasar, page 28*

If that be the case then one redundant generation has been added to the genealogy.

Controversy No. 2:   ***Imam's son born in the house of a missionary.***

On page 253, Noorum Mubin records: One day Imam Muhtadi became sick. He invited his chief missionary *(Dai)* Muhammad to see him. (Muhammad was son of *Dai* Kiya Buzurgumid, who was an heir of Hasan-i Sabbah, the famous *'Old Man of the Mountain'*.) Imam told *Dai* Muhammad to take his (Imam's) pregnant wife to his house (Dai's house) and take care of her. Imam Muhtadi prophesied that his wife will deliver a male child, and the Dai should raise the child like a Prince in his (Dai's) house and later on declare him as Imam after him. Imam gave 'Sanad' (documents) to **his wife**. Thereafter Imam went into seclusion and lived the life of a *Dervish* (mystic).

These are the circumstances under which, according to the Ismaili sources, **Imam Qahir was born in the house of a missionary (Dai)**.

One day (*after 36 years*), the child of the prophecy that was born and raised in the house of Dai, was presented by Dai Muhammad as Imam Qahir, before Alamutian Ismailis.

The Noorum Mubin records on page 255 and 256 that the congregants demanded proof of the child's legitimacy to the throne of Imamat. Dai asked **his wife** to produce the 'Sanad' which Imam Muhtadi had given to **her**. In spite of that, many of the congregants expressed open resentment and indignation at Dai's declaration. On page 256, Noorum Mubin records this revolt lasted for 5 years and thereafter Imam Qahir became a fullfledged established Imam. Noorum Mubin also records that Imam Qahir became Imam in 552 A.H. and died in 557 A.H. His Imamat lasted five years (*the revolt also lasted five years*). Noorum Mubin has recorded details of the prophecy, the birth of an Imam's son into the house of a Dai, giving of 'Sanad', as well as of the declaration and of the revolt, but has not recorded the year of births for Muhtadi and Qahir.

Note:

1. Abualy records, Imam Qahir was born in 1121. He became Imam in 1157. That makes him 36 years old when he was declared as Imam Qahir by Dai Muhammad. It is strange that Alamutians did not know for 36 years who was this child and who was his father!

2. Ismailis of Alamut demanded 'Sanad' as proof of his legitimacy. Why did they keep on revolting after the production of the 'Sanad' (documents)?

3. On page 253 Noorum Mubin writes the 'Sanad' was given by **Imam Muhtadi to his wife**. On page 256, Noorum Mubin writes the **Dai asked his wife** to produce the 'Sanad' which Imam gave **to her**. Did Imam Mutadi's wife marry Dai Muhammad and become Dai's wife, within that period of 36 years?

Non-Ismaili sources claim that the entire 'story' of Imam Hadi's escape from the prison, his subsequent marriage in Iran, birth of Hadi's son Muhtadi, Muhtadi living his life in seclusion, prophecy by Muhtadi, and the birth of Muhtadi's son in the house of a Dai and the upbringing of that child as Prince in complete seclusion by Dai Muhammad is a fabrication, to link up the ancestry of the Dai's son Hasan with Imam Nizar.

On page 258, Noorum Mubin has recorded the declaration of Imamat by a false claimant, during the period of Imam Qahir's Imamat (between 552 and 557 A.H.). Noorum Mubin writes that the name of the false claimant was Hasan and he was the **son of Dai Muhammad.**

Controversy No. 3:   **"Two Hasans"**

1. Noorum Mubin records that the child of the Prophecy (*Qahir*) that was born and raised in the house of Dai Muhammad, had a son and the name of that child was Hasan.

2. Noorum Mubin **also** records that Dai Muhammad had a son which he raised in his own house, and the name of that child was **also** Hasan.

Ismaili sources claim it is a coincidence that both the children were named Hasan, both had claimed the Imamat, and both were born in the house of Dai Muhammad.

Non-Ismaili sources reject the *story* of **"Two Hasans."** They have recorded only one Hasan, the son of Dai Muhammad.

Imam Ala-Zikrihis-Salam, the 23rd Generation:

Controversy No.1:

"Ala Zikrihis-salam" is not a name, it is a terminology. The literal translation of *"ala Zikrihis-salam"* is "Upon his mention be peace." In the history of the Assassins and Alamut, this terminology has been associated with the person that made the Declaration of Qiyama.

In 1957/58, Professor W. Ivanow surveyed the enclave of Alamut, the site where this Historical Proclamation for 'The Great Resurrection' (Qiyama), was made. Ivanow's report of the survey was published by the Ismaili Society, Tehran in 1960. On page 28 of the survey report entitled *'Alamut and Lamasar'*, Professor Ivanow writes:

> "In the Ismaili terminology this kind of blessing, 'blessing be upon his mention,' is used in connection with the mention of the Qaim, the Ismaili term for Mahdi of the day of Resurrection, who is expected, thus belonging to the future, and his real name still remaining unknown. It may be para-

phrased as: 'Blessings be upon Him, whatever name He may have.' There is another version (particularly much used in Druze texts), which is more complex: li-dhikri-hi's-sujud-wa't-tasbih, that is, 'prostration and glorification be due upon His mention."

On page 269, Noorum Mubin has recorded that "ala-Zikrihis-Salam" was a 'Lakab' (term) used by Muhtadi, Qahir and Hasan. Ismaili historians have recorded the name of their 23rd Imam as Hasan, ala-Zikrihis-Salam. In the Book of 'Dua', there is no mention of the name "Hasan". Ismailis recite "ala-Zikrihis-Salam" – a terminology – as the 23rd Imam in their "Dua". In other words, the name of the 23rd Imam was **unknown or doubtful** to the author of 'Dua'.

Controversy No. 2:

According to Ismaili sources, the two Hasans were contemporaneous in so many respects that even a fairy tale may sound more realistic. Below is a table of historical records of 'TWO HASANS'.

		HASAN descendant of *Imam* Nizar	HASAN descendant of *Dai* Buzurgumid
1.	Name ...	HASAN	HASAN
2.	Birth ...	1126/1127 *	1127
3.	Death ...	1166	1166
4.	Son's Name	ala-Muhammad	Muhammad II
5.	Son's Birth ...	1147*	1147
6.	Father's Death	1162	1162

* As per Ismailia Association for Pakistan's Gujrati history book *'Ismaili Imamono Toonk Itihas', Part 3 – 1975.*

Controversy No. 3:

On the 17th day of Ramadan, 559 A.H. (8 August 1164) – the anniversary of the murder of Hazrat Ali – a certain Hasan, wearing a white garment and white turban came down from a castle and stood up on a raised pulpit and made the following Historical Declaration, holding his sword:

> "The Imam of our time has sent you his blessing and his compassion, and has called you his special chosen servants. He has freed you from the burden of the rules of Holy Law (Shari'a), and has brought you to the Resurrection (Qiyama)."
>
> *'The Assassins' page 72*
> *Al Saqi Books-1985*

Almost all the leading historians have recorded that the above Declaration was made by Hasan, the son of Dai Muhammad.

Ismaili historians have claimed that the said Declaration was made by Hasan, son of Qahir, who was the legitimate claimant. The other Hasan (son of Dai Mohammad) had claimed the Imamat, but had not declared the above Declaration.

Continuing the text of the Declaration recorded, Professor Bernard Lewis writes:

> "In addition, the Imam named Hasan, the son of Muhammad, the son of Buzurgumid, as 'our vicar, da'i and proof. Our party must obey and follow him both in religious and worldly matters, recognize his commands as binding, and know that his word is our word."
>
> *'The Assassins' page 72*

Historians have also recorded that after this public manifestation, Hasan son of Dai Muhammad circulated writings in which he said that while outwardly he was known as the grandson of Buzurgumid, in the esoteric reality he was the Imam of the time. Some had argued that Hasan was not claiming physical descent from the Fatimid Imams but a kind of *Spiritual Filiation* (esoteric descent). Since he had declared *Qiyama* (the age of Resurrection), the significance of a physical descent had ceased to be of concern. After his death, his son Muhammad II confirmed himself and his father as the descendants of the Fatimid Imams. Professor Marshall G.S. Hodgson writes:

> "He (Hasan's son) established Hasan as imam in the fullest sense, and not merely the representative of the imam, thus changing the very genealogy of the family. ... Hasan received a good Fatimid genealogy. Once Hasan and therefore his son Mohammad (II) was endowed with an 'Alid genealogy, the breach with the time when there were only dai's in Alamut was complete, and the new dispensation inaugurated with all propriety."
>
> *'The Order of Assassins'*
> *page 160-Mouton & Co. 1955*

Controversy No. 4:

Noorum Mubin records, Hasan ala Zikrihis-Salam was born in 1114. If that was the year of birth for the 23rd Imam, then we have a very unique situation in the history of Ismaili Imams. A biological improbability.

From Noorum Mubin we get the following data:

Imam No. 18 died in ...	1094 A.D.
Imam No. 19 and 20 went into prison in ...	1094 (or later)
Imam No. 20 escaped from the prison, married and had a son in ...	1094 (or later)
Imam No. 21, year of birth unknown	...
Imam No. 22, year of birth unknown	...
Imam No. 23, year of birth ...	1114

From the above we know that the time difference between marriage of 20th Imam and birth of 23rd Imam is 1114 minus 1094 = **20 years (or less).**

How can a person get married, have a son, a grandson and a great grandson within 20 years? Ismaili historians had no alternative but to say that the book of Ismaili history, recommended by their Imam, was inaccurate and fallacious.

Controversy No. 5:

In 1935, Noorum Mubin recorded that the birth of **23rd** Imam was in **1114 A.D.** In 1974, Abualy recorded that the birth of **22nd** Imam (father of 23rd Imam) was in **1121A.D.**

If Abualy did not move the above birth date of 23rd Imam then his book of history would show that the 23rd Imam was **born 7 years BEFORE his father**. He rejected the date recorded by his sister source and wrote that the birth date recorded by Noorum Mubin was incorrect. He moved the date by **38 years** and wrote: the **23rd Imam** was born in **1152.**

In the process, Abualy may have overlooked the fact that he had recorded the birth year of **24th** Imam as **1155.** In other words he recorded that the son (the 24th Imam) was born when his father was only three years old. In 1987, I enquired from Abualy about the above mentioned discrepancy in the date. I was also interested in knowing from him, if he had any records or sources from which he had copied these dates. Abualy chose not to answer my letter.

Controversy No. 6:

In 1974, Abualy recorded that the birth of **23rd** Imam was in **1152 A.D.** In 1975, Ismailia Association for Pakistan recorded that the birth of **24th** Imam was in **1147**.

If the Ismailia Association for Pakistan was to confirm the date recorded by Abualy (1152 A.D.) for the 23rd Imam, then their history book would show that the son (the 24th Imam) was born five years **BEFORE his father**. They dismissed the dates recorded by Noorum Mubin and Abualy. The Ismailia Association for Pakistan wrote, 23rd Imam was born in **1126/27** A.D. (page 19-part 3).

This new date of birth (1126/27) for Hasan, son of Imam Qahir **COINCIDES** with the birth date of HASAN, son of Dai Muhammad.

Controversy No. 7:

When was HASAN, ala Zikrihis-Salam, the son of Imam Qahir, born according to Ismaili sources?

1. *'Noorum-Mubin'* (1935-India) records **1114 A.D.**

2. *'A Brief History of Ismailism'* (1974-Africa) records **1152 A.D.**

3. *'Toonk Itihas'* (1975-Pakistan) records **1126/27 A.D.**

4. *'History of Ismaili Imams'* (1976-Canada) written by Al-Waiz Hasan Nazerali of Toronto records **1131 A.D.**

Non-Ismaili historians do not confirm his existence in history, as such, no dates are recorded for his birth.

Note: Every country has its own date for the birth of an Imam whose entity in history is so doubtful.

Controversy No. 8:

In the history of *Assassins* (Ismailis of Alamut), the historical Declaration of *Qiyama* – **'The Great Resurrection'** – made by Hasan, the *Qaimul Qiyama* (Bringer of the Resurrection), has been recorded by Ismaili as well as non-Ismaili sources, as a most significant event in the history. It marked the end of time, lifting of the veil of concealment and abrogation of the Religious Laws – *the Islamic Shari'a.* In the middle of the day, in the middle of the holy month of Islamic fasting, Hasan, the Bringer of the Resurrection, standing on a pulpit facing the congregants, with their backs toward Mecca, ordered breaking of the fast and joining with him in the afternoon banquet, drinking of wine and merry-making. Hasan had invited Ismailis from the neighbouring fortresses into the courtyard of the Alamut for this special occasion.

Professor Peter Lamborn Wilson writes: "Alamut broke its fast forever and proclaimed perpetual holiday" (*'Scandal', page 39*).

This tradition still exists amongst Ismailis. They do enjoy the freedom from fasting, during the month declared for fasting by Allah (S.W.T.), in the Quran. In the past, the 11th Imam "Mahdi" had abolished *Hajj* during his Imamat. This time, the Lord of the Resurrection, Hasan; abolished the entire Laws of Shari'a. This abolition of *Shari'a* and institution of *Qiyama* is the base of esoterism *(Batiniyat)* of Ismailism. Abualy has recorded the text of the Declaration on page 73, as under:

"Today I have explained to you the Law (shari'at) and its meaning. **I make you free** from the rigidity of the Law and resurrect you from the bondage of the letter to the freedom of the spirit of the Law. **Obey me and follow my farma'n**. Give up all your misunderstanding and be united. Lead a virtuous life to be free from the fear of the Day of Judgement. Union with God, in reality, is the resurrection. **Break your fast and rejoice**. This is the day of utmost happiness and gratitude."

Here are a few important questions, to which any believing Muslim would like to have answers. Did Prophet Muhammad (s.a.s.) possess an authority to revoke, substitute or abrogate permanently the God given Quranic Laws, specially of Hajj *(Q.3/97)* and of Fastings *(Q.2/183)*? Could the Prophet have authorized his representative *(Ali)* to do so? Does the Quran authorize anyone to substitute, revoke or abrogate the Quranic Laws, especially the Five Pillars of Islam? The text of the historical Declaration reads **"I make you free"**. Who is **"I"**? It is immaterial whether HASAN made the Declaration as a descendant of Nizar or descendant of Buzurgumid. Whether he made the Declaration as an Imam or as a representative of a hidden Imam (as most of the historians have recorded), the question is who gave or wherefrom **"I"** got the authority to liberate and set free Ismailis from the rigidity of the Law. Anyone who blindly obeys such a Declaration and consider himself or herself as "FREE" and then behaves as an *"Unbound Muslim"* without knowing answers to the above questions and without verifying the authority and authenticity of the **"I"**, is certainly treading a path which could lead him or her to a place where no Muslim *(one who submits to Allah)* would like to be on the Day of Judgement. **"I"** had not only equated himself with the Revealer of the Quran but had superseded Him by rescinding His Laws *(nauzbillah)*. Think for a moment, should a true Muslim be obeying *al-Mahdi* (the 11th Imam), or *al-Mu'id* (the One Who reproduces life)? OR, obeying *al-Hasan* (the 23rd Imam) or *al-Hasib* (the One Who takes account of everything)?

Controversy No. 9:

Ismaili sources claim; HASAN-the descendant of **Imam** Nizar, made the Historical Declaration two years after the death of his father, *Imam* Qahir.

Non-Ismaili sources claim; HASAN-the descendant of **Dai** Buzurgumid, made the Historical Declaration two years after the death of his father, *Dai* Muhammad.

Notes:

1. If **Imam** Hasan was the declarer of the Declaration and a designated son of the previous Imam, then he should have declared himself Imam, immediately after the death of his father. As per over a thousand year old Ismaili tradition and practice, the seat of *Imamat* could not remain vacant for two years. Someone has to receive the *Zakat* money and perform the Jamati ceremonies of forgiving sins, etc.

2. It is an Ismaili custom, prevalent to this day, that immediately after the death of an Imam, his designated successor is installed to the throne of the Imamat, by the *Jamat* (community). Thereafter, each and every member of the Jamat takes *'Baiyat'* (oath of allegiance) by kissing the hand of their new Imam. Whereas, on the day of the Historical Declaration, Hasan made the announcement and declared himself "Imam-e-Zaman", as per Ismaili sources; "Vicar,

Dai and Proof *(Hujjah)*" as per non-Ismaili sources. There is no mention of a ceremony of an Installation of an Imam to the throne of Imamat, nor of 'Baiyat' ceremony, instead Hasan asked the Jamat to join him in a banquet and merry-making.

3. The important question is why did Hasan circulate a writing to the Ismailis that he was Imam-e-Zaman? If he was a son of the previous Imam, who had died two years ago, then Ismailis would have already known him as their Imam-e-Zaman.

4. In the end part of the Ismaili prayers, Ismailis recite the name of their *Hazar* (present) Imam. The question is: Did the Assassins recite "ala-Zikrihis salaam" or "Hasan"? If they recited "Hasan" the circular was not warranted. If they recited the term "ala-Zikrihis salaam", **as the Ismailis do today**, then the name of that individual was not known, because he was non existent and whose manifestation was being awaited, as recorded by Professor W. Ivanow. Ismaili historians changed the history but could not change the genealogy, in the book of prayer.

Imam Ruknuddin Khair Shah, the 27th Generation:

Controversy No. 1:

Imam Ruknuddin was the last Ismaili Imam of the Alamut. Mongolian soldiers of Halaku Khan destroyed every house and building in Alamut, conquered and demolished Ismaili castles of Alamut, and of the surrounding areas. They massacred almost every Ismaili and brought an end to the Ismaili Empire by 1258 A.D. Abualy writes:

"At last by treachery and tricks the Mongols defeated the Ismailis and destroyed whatever could be destroyed ... Thirty thousand Ismailis were killed in one day during this war of Alamut. Altogether eighty thousand Ismailis sacrificed their lives for the sake of their faith and their Imam in the battles of Alamut."

(page 77)

Noorum-Mubin records that babies that were sleeping in the cradles were also killed. In the words of Bernard Lewis, a well known historian of that era, Ata Malik Juvayni (1226–83), writes:

"He (Ruknuddin) and his followers were kicked to a pulp and then put to the sword; and of him and his stock no trace was left, and he and his kindred became but a tale on men's lips and a tradition in the world."

'The Assassins' page 95

Similar accounts have also been recorded by other historians of that period, viz. Rashid al–Din Fadlallah (c. 1247–1318) and Abu'l Qasim Kashani – a contemporary of Rashid. Ismaili sources claim that this was the end of Ismaili domain in Alamut but the records of Juvayni are not to be trusted. Few Ismailis survived the massacre and amongst them was a son of Imam Ruknuddin who was sent outside of the Alamut by his father, before the attack. This son continued the line of Imamat. Some of the Ismaili sources write the next 3 generations of Ruknuddin continued the Imamat in **Iraq**. Others say they were residing in **Iran**.

Non-Ismaili sources claim there are no records available to substantiate that claim for Imamat having survived the massacre. The Ismaili history books are devoid of vital data for the next eighteen generations of Ruknuddin. Even the latest history book of Ismaili Imams in Gujrati published by the Ismailia Association for Pakistan in 1980, has no records of the year of birth of their Imams, starting from Imam number 28 to number 46 (the Aga Khan I).

Ismaili sources claim, the period starting from the fall of Alamut to the Aga Khan I is known as *"Dawr-al-satr'* (period of the hiding). Imams were living in concealments and as such, very little is known about them.

Non-Ismaili sources are astonished to find that appointments of dozens of Pirs and Dais by these Imams of *"Dawr-al-satr"* are recorded by Ismaili historians. Detailed activities of these alleged appointees and their frequent visits from India to pay *Zakat* money to their Imams are recorded. The so claimed regular visits of hundreds of Ismailis from India, to pay homage to their beloved Spiritual Father (*Imams*), are recorded by Abualy and other Ismaili historians. Why is it that none of these alleged Dais, Pirs, and visitors had taken any note of the year of birth of any one of the dozens of children born to the spouses of their Imam, for over a period of **five centuries**? Contrary to this, the years of their becoming Imams is recorded by all the Ismaili sources, for each and every one of them.

Ismailis of Syria were surprised to hear that a descendant of their Imams in Alamut, had settled himself in India. A delegation of Syrian Ismailis came to see the Aga Khan in India. Aga Khan gave these Syrian Ismailis the Gujrati *Dua* (Ismaili Prayer), containing a genealogy of Ismaili Imams from Hazrat Ali to Aga Khan. These Arab Ismailis of Syria had difficulties of pronouncing the text in Gujrati, but they continued praying in Gujrati, because it was the Farman of their Imam. Finally, they requested for a Dua (prayer) in Arabic. At the end of his Imamat, Aga Khan III gave the Arabic Dua to the entire community.

Controversy No. 2:

One Ismaili source contradicts the other.

Abualy writes on page 77:

> "... he (Ruknuddin) was murdered by the Mongols, on the twenty-ninth of Shawwal, 654 A.H. (**19th of November, 1256**)."

On page 140, Ismailia Association for Pakistan records that Ruknuddin married a Tatar (Mongol) lady and then went to Karakoram, the capital of the Mongol Empire, on 1st Rabbial Awal, 655 A.H. (**9th of March, 1257**) to see Emperor Manaku Khan (The Emperor refused to see the Imam, so he returned back, disappointed).

Note: Died in November, but married and went to Karakoram, four months **later**?

Imam Shamsuddin Muhammad, the 28th Generation:

Ismaili historians have already mystified the readers with the perplexity of "Two Hasans" in the history of their 23rd Imam. This time they have tangled "Three Shams" with even greater riddle. They are admitting the fact that there has been lots of confusion, missing dates, mixed up names and data in connection with these three personalities.

1. **Imam** – Shamsuddin Muhammad, the 28th Imam

2. **Saint** – Shams, the Murshid (mentor) of Jalaluddin Rumi

3. Pir – Shams of Multan

In section one of this chapter we will try to identify these "three Shams" by their names, places of residence, and historical backgrounds.

In the second section we will try to compare the dates of their births, dates of historical events connected with them and the years of their deaths.

Section One

1. Imam Shams: the 28th Imam

History records that the son of the 27th Imam was named Muhammad. He had no son by the name of Shams or Shamsuddin.

Ismaili historians confirm that his name was Muhammad; but they have added, that later on he was known as Shams (*Sun*) because he was very handsome (page 308 "Noorum-Mubin"). Ismaili historians claim that Muhammad, son of Imam Ruknuddin, escaped the mass killing by Mongols and continued the Imamat in Azerbaijan, Iran. This report of his residence is *self contradicted*. Below are the extracts taken from "Noorum-Mubin":

1. On page 309 it records that after the destruction of Alamut, the 28th Imam escaped from the hands of his enemies. He survived and lived as a *Dervish* (Mystic) and that fact was known only to his family members, *Dais* (missionaries) and *Fidais* (devout followers). Lady members of his family did the embroidery works and Imam used to sell them. He was known as *"Zardoz"* (an embroiderer). Ismailis used to visit their Imam for *"Baiyat"* (oath of allegiance)

in **Azerbaijan**, where Imam used to live.

2. On page 317 quoting from a booklet which had survived the Baluchi revolt and was found by the publisher recently from the town of "Zarka,' the "Noorum-Mubin' writes that the records preserved in this booklet conclusively prove that Mawlana Imam Shamsuddin Muhammad (the 28th Imam) used to reside in privacy with his uncle, Shahin Shah, in **Tabriz** and used to do the work of embroidery.

Note: In the first edition of Noorum-Mubin published in 1936, there is no record of this booklet found at "Zarka." This information appears in the third edition of Noorum-Mubin, which was published in 1951 by the Ismailia Association for India. The information contained in this booklet could have been found by the Ismailia Association between the period 1936 and 1951. The author has recorded the name of the town as "Zarka" but the correct name of the town is "Zirukh" and it is located near the city of Hyderabad, in the Province of Sind, Pakistan, on a bank of the river Indus. The Baluchi Revolt mentioned by the author was the revolt led by Baluchi leader Mir Sher Muhammad Khan of Baluchistan against the British Raj in 1843. Aga Khan I, a leader of Ismaili **Muslims**, took the side of the British Raj and offered the services of his followers and himself to **Christian** General-Sir Charles Napier, to fight and defeat the Baluchi **Muslims**. In retaliation, Mir Sher Muhammad Khan attacked the army of Aga Khan, in the town of Zirukh, which was the *Darkhana* of Ismailis in Sind. Noorum-Mubin has recorded that 70 Ismailis died fighting on that night. Aga Khan I, the 46th Imam, saved his life by fleeing on a horse in his nightshirt. During his flight he fell from his horse, lost his four teeth and became unconscious. He was then carried by his followers to Hyderabad.

3. On page 306, Noorum-Mubin writes:

> "Even today in the fort of Alamut (ruins of Alamut) there is a house built of stone and mud. It has a wooden door. The people residing in the area believe that the tomb within the house is of some **"Imamzada"** (son of an Imam).

2. Saint Shams

Noorum Mubin records on page 309, that Saint Shams was the son of Imam Ala-uddin Muhammad, the 26th Imam. He was *Murshid*(mentor) of famous mystic poet Mawlana Jalaluddin Rumi. Saint Shams was the uncle of Imam Shams. Some Ismaili historians have recorded that Imam Shams was **also** Murshid of Mawlana Rumi. Noorum Mubin records that Saint Shams was known as Shams Tabrizi because he lived in Tabriz. The booklet found in "Zarka" records that Imam Shams **also** lived in Tabriz.

On page 316, Noorum Mubin has quoted a couple of verses of Rumi. In relation to these verses, Noorum Mubin has recorded that Mawlana Rumi stopped his preaching in the ecstasy of love for his "Murshid," the Holy Imam(Shams), and began writing poems. The verse quoted by Noorum Mubin is an elaborate discourse which says, Shams the *Zahir* (manifest) Imam, the friend of Allah, with whom is sustained this world, this period, the earth and sky. The Imam's self is sinless, glorious and to be worshipped, etc.

Such records give indication that the **son of the 26th Imam**, who used to live in Tabriz and whose real name was Shams became "Imam Shams" as well as the Murshid of Mawlana Rumi. The **son of the 27th Imam,** whose real name was Muhammad, did not become the 28th Imam. The tomb located in the ruins of Alamut, which is called a tomb of some *"Imamzada"* (son of an Imam) could be the tomb of that Muhammad.

3. **Pir Shams** of Multan

The so called "Pir" Shams of Multan was neither an Ismaili nor a "Pir" of Ismailis. He was not sent to India by a post Alamut Imam, Qasim Shah, or his son – Islam Shah. He came to Multan, India, about 50 years before the fall of Alamut. The claim that he was a Pir and sent by a post Alamut Imam is not only baseless but has been instituted to give credibility to the genealogy of the post Alamut Imams whose history itself has been an enigmatic saga.

Shah Shams of Multan was a Muslim Saint. His life has been an open book. He has hundreds of thousands of adherents residing in Pakistan, India, Tibet and Kashmir. Most of these are Sunni Muslims and not Ismailis. This fact is being confirmed by Noorum Mubin. His shrine is in the city of Multan, Pakistan. The *Mutawalli* (custodian) of the shrine has a *Shajra* (genealogical tree). We will compare the dates recorded in the Shajra of his birth, arrival in Multan and death, in the second part of this section. He was born in Ghazni (Afghanistan) and not in Shabzwar or Tabriz in Iran. He was born about 100 years before the destruction of the forts of Alamut by Halaku Khan.

It is interesting to know that Ismaili historians contradict each other and the Ismaili Ginans, composed by Pirs, contradict the Ismaili historians regarding the identity of Pir Shams:

Noorum Mubin records on page 324:

"An Ismaili Dai that came to India who is also commonly known as Dai Hazrat **Shams Tabrizi is Pir Shams**. His genealogy is: Hazrat Shamshuddin bin Salaudin bin Salehdin ... etc., etc. Pir Shams' father was **follower** of Imam Shamsuddin Muhammad, the *"Zardoz"*(Embroiderer). He was also a propagator of Ismaili faith."

On page 120, Abualy records in his book *'A Brief History of Ismaili Imams'*:

"During the one hundred and eighteen years of his life, Pir Shams converted over half a million disciples in many countries. Pir Shams was Shams Sabzwari and **not Shams Tabriz** who was the Master of Jalaluddin Rumi. Shams Tabriz was the **son** of Imam Alauddin Mohammed and brother of Imam Ruknuddin Khorshah. Both were Ismaili saints. They were contemporaries."

Note: If Pir Shams was an Ismaili saint, what happened to those half a million disciples? Today, seven centuries later, that number could have grown into millions of "Shamsi Ismailis." Why did they give up the Unique Ismaili Tariqah and become Sunni Muslims?

Upon study of Ismaili Ginan *"Satveniji Vel"* composed by Nar Muhammad Shah, we find that Imam Shamsuddin abdicated his Imamat in favour of his son, Qasim Shah, and came to India as an Ismaili Dai. This Ginan indicates that Imam Shams of Iraq (or Iran) was the same person who is known as Pir Shams of India. Some Ismaili historians refute this Ginanic claim and write that Nar Muhammad Shah had an ulterior motive behind this fabrication. One Ismaili missionary, whose text is recorded below writes: Imam Shams was "Saint Shams" and also "Pir Shams". Imam Shams wrote the *"Garbis"* (folk songs in Gujrati) and *Ginans* in Punjabi.

My father Itmadi Ebrahim and grandfather Alijah Rajan Meherally were devout followers of Aga Khan and also leading members of the Ismailia community. My father performed the weighing ceremony of Aga Khan III with diamonds, upon his Diamond Jubilee in 1947, in Bombay. My grandfather had accompanied Late Pir Subzali on a perilous mission of *"Dawah"*(preaching and conversion) from India to Pamir through Badakshan in the high mountains of Northern India. My grandfather died in the 1930's and I inherited his collection of religious books. One of the books that I liked to read over and over again, in those days was *'Vedic Islam'*. It was written by my grandfather's friend, Al-Waiz Ebrahim Jusab Varteji. He was a highly respected missionary and my teacher. He devoted his life doing research on Shiaism. On page 348 of his book, Missionary Varteji writes:

> "After the fall of Alamut, Shamshuddin Muhammad became Imam. In the history books he is known as Shams Tabrizi. Mawlana Rumi did *Baiyat* of Shamshuddin Muhammad and only after that, he became the Master of Knowledge. Similarly in Punjab there are Shamsi Ismailis who also got their knowledge from him. In Gujrat, his *Garbis* (Songs in Gujrati) were instrumental in the destruction of Hindu idols. He was the son of Mawlana Ruknuddin Khorshah and his descendant is the Aga Khan III, the author of *'India in Transition'*, which is like a "Gita of Shree Krishna."

Section Two

1. Imam Shams: the 28th Imam

Abualy contradicts himself twice!

Birth: Ismailia Association for India and Pakistan have not recorded his year of birth.

Abualy writes on page 78, that he was born in 1250 A.D. He then contradicts himself in the same paragraph, when he writes: "Mowlana Imam Shamsuddin succeeded his father at the age of eight;" and (in the heading) he writes, his Imamat began from **1256 A.D.** 1250 + 8 = **1258 A.D.** (not 1256).

Death: On page 79, Abualy writes that the Holy Imam died in **1310 A.D.** But, he contradicts himself by writing on page 78: "His Imamat lasted fifty-six years." 1256 + 56 = **1312 A.D.** (not 1310).

2. Saint Shams: the Murshid of Rumi

Birth: Ismaili sources have no record.

Death: Ismailia Association for Pakistan and India have recorded the year of death as 1247 A.D. Abualy has not recorded the date.

Note: According to the above recorded date, Saint Shams died when Imam Shams was not yet born (birth 1250). The question therefore is who was "Imam Shams" in whose ecstasy Rumi wrote the poems quoted by Noorum Mubin?

3. Pir Shams of Multan:

Birth: The Sajrah with the *Mutawalli* (custodian) of the shrine records his birth in Ghazni in 1165 A.D.

Abualy records 1241 A.D. A difference of **76 years**. Other Ismaili sources record 1244 A.D.

Arrival in Multan: The Sajrah records his arrival in Multan in 1201 A.D. Abualy writes he was appointed as "Pir" by Imam Shams (birth 1250). Other Ismaili sources claim he was appointed by Imam Qasim Shah (son of Imam Shams). Ginans written in Gujrati have two dates of his arrival in India. Ginan *"Surbhan"* writes 1118 A.D. and Ginan *"Chandrabhan"* records his arrival in Chenab, India, in 1143 A.D.

Note: Both these Ginans are supposed to have been composed by Pir Shams as per Ismaili tradition and beliefs.

Death: The Sajrah records his death in 1276 A.D.

Ismaili sources record 1356 A.D., a difference of **80 years**.

Ismaili historians and Ginans have recorded that Pir Shams had an encounter with Shaikh Baha'oddin Zakariyah Multani during his visit to the city of Multan (for details please refer to chapter 6). The Shaikh Baha'oddin died in 1276 A.D., hence the date of Pir Shams' death recorded by Ismaili sources (1356 A.D.) does not make him contemporary of the Shaikh. Furthermore, Shaikh Baha'oddin was Master of Fakhroddin Ibrahim al-Iraqi, who died in Damascus in 1289 A.D. Pir Shams, Shaikh Baha'oddin and Fakhroddin Iraqi were contemporaries and died in 1276, 1276, and 1289 A.D., respectively.

Imam Abul Hasanali, the 44th Generation:

Ismaili sources conspicuously contradict each other.

On page 90 of his book, "A Brief History of Ismailism," Abualy writes under the heading "Imam Abul Hasanali":

> "When Nadir Shah invaded India, in January 1739, **he requested the Holy Imam to accompany him in order to bring good luck.** The Holy Imam went with the Shah but returned home after the conquest of Lahore."

Reproduced below is the original Gujrati text from the history book of Ismaili Imams published by H.R.H. The Aga Khan Ismailia Association for Pakistan (page 188); which blatantly contradicts the above record.

નાદિરશાહ સુન્ની અકીદાના મુસ્લિમ હતા. તેણે ઇરાનના શીઆ ઇસ્ના-અશારી લોકો ઉપર ઝુલમ કરવાનું શરૂ કર્યું. થોડા સમય પછી તે કિરમાન આવ્યો અને ત્યાંના સૂફી સંપ્રદાયના લોકો ઉપર દમનનો કોરડો વીંઝવા લાગ્યો. તેણે હઝરત ઇમામ શાહ અબુલ હસનઅલી (અ.સ.)ને કેદ કર્યા અને પૂરા મૂલકમાં જુલ્મો સિતમની આગ ભડકાવી દીધી.

Translation of the Gujrati text:

"Nadir Shah was a Sunni Muslim by faith. He began the persecution of Iranian citizens of Shia Ithna'ashri faith. After some time he came to Kirman and committed extreme brutality with the local Sufi population. **He imprisoned Hazrat Imam Shah Hasanali (a.s.)** and engulfed the entire country with his fire of atrocities."

The glaring contradictions recorded above are not from an ancient history. Imam Abul-Hasan Ali's Imamat was only 250 years ago, from 1730 to 1780 A.D. Both the sources are Ismaili and are published in the 1980's. Both cannot be telling the truth. So, whom do you trust?

"Ismaili History is not to be Trusted"

In the words of Professor Peter Lamborn Wilson:

"Ismaili history is not to be trusted – a tangle of bloodlines and feuds, attacks by ignorant heresimachs. But Ismaili *story* can be trusted whether it is literally true or not, because the very nature of what is taught or told ensures and necessitates a transmutation into 'myth'. Marco Polo's tall-tale of the drugged devotees is certainly not meaningless, even though told by an outsider. The fable of the childhood pact made by Omar Khayyam, Hasan-i Sabbah and the Nizam al-Mulk is also an outsider's romance, but not without significance. The story that the last Old Man of the Mountain became the wandering dervish Shams of Tabriz (Rumi's spiritual companion) is historically impossible but resonant with hints and clues.

"Finally, the most trustworthy stories are those traceable to the Assassins themselves. The story of the Qiyamat revolves around its central image, the mandala marked out by four cosmic banners surrounding a pulpit ... the blackrobed figure with raised sword ... the mountain fortress in the background, umber and ochre and grey ... the circle of warrior-scholars with their wine-cups, breaking the sacred fast of Ramazan ... the cobalt-blue desert sky ...

"This mandala breaks loose from the moorings of its historical setting, and even from the text in which it is embedded. It becomes a complex of images, an Emblem, which can be located in the consciousness and expanded, brought to life as an integral element in one's own individual story — the personal myth which always comprises a movement from unawareness toward realization.

"Meditation thus becomes narration. The symbols one penetrates make up the path one follows, as with the Grail knights, whose adventures were subjected to the ta'wil of the forest hermits.

"The outward physical-historical Alamut, the 'hidden garden' where devotees were freed of State and Church, tax, dogma and Law — this image perhaps cannot be imposed on the 'real world', was perhaps but a fleeting vision, even in Alamut itself. It is amusing to speculate about the possibility of experimenting with some of the practical teachings of Alamut in the context of today's world. But even if the social freedom of an Alamut cannot be attained, this in no way lessens the importance of the personal freedom granted by the interiorization of the Alamut-story, and of the Qiyamat.

"Ultimately society and Law can do nothing to impinge on this freedom — except to hang the free man from a gibbet in Baghdad. You are already free, says the Lord of the Resurrection. So there exists no other story worth living, whatever the risk."

*"Scandal", 1988, Autonomedia Inc., N.Y.,
pages 54-55*

Peter Lamborn Wilson is the former editor of Sophia Perennis, the journal of the Iranian Academy of Philosophy; author and translator of numerous books on Islamic, Sufi, and Spiritual themes. He is also an Honourary Fellow of the Muhyiddin Ibn Arabi Society and co-editor of Semiotexte (e).

Allah says:

"The parable of those who take protectors other than Allah is that of the Spider, who builds (to itself) a house; but truly the flimsiest of houses is the Spider's house, if they but knew. Verily Allah doth know of (everything) whatever that they call upon besides Him; and He is Exalted (in power), Wise. And such are the parables We set for mankind but only those understand them who have knowledge."

Holy Quran 29/41 to 43

The knowledge has come. Will they understand now?

"And say: 'Truth has (now) arrived and Falsehood has vanished away; for Falsehood is (by its nature) bound to vanish'."

Holy Quran 17/81

12

Unique Beliefs

Reality and Reliance

You are reading this sentence – that is a reality to you. I wrote it – that is a reality to me, but for you, it is a matter of reliance. My signature on the book is the basis of your reliance. Similarly, the realities behind the tenets or creeds of a religion are what give it credence and support. Based upon the level of reliance one has and where one places it, one becomes a Jew, a Christian, a Muslim or an Ismaili.

A man of religion rejuvenates his faith and becomes devout when his reliance meets with affirmative responses. When the faith overtakes the realities, however, the religion transforms itself into a blind faith or a cult. Here the man of religion has given up his power of reasoning. The authorship of a book can be established without even showing the signature on the book. Falsehoods, fictions and fabrications can be traded as Realities and Reliabilities. The faith can now be distorted and moulded at the whims and wishes of the dictator of tenet. There is a Farman of Aga Khan III wherein he says;

> "If I say it is night, (you are to believe) it is night. If I say it is day, (you are to believe) it is day."

Reliance or faith must be based upon Truth. Faith is a synonym for religion. Hence, a religion must be based upon Truth if it is to survive. When the so-called realities and beliefs of a religion are exposed or unclothed and what manifests itself is the falsity, then the realities become fiction. The blind faith or trust receives an unexpected setback and the so called religion comes to a violent end. History has recorded many such cults that have appeared and then disappeared along with their directors, from the face of this earth. The most recent one is that of Reverend Jim Jones of Guyana.

There is a fine line, drawn between religion and cult. A religion that tells you to sacrifice your mind and then commit yourself with emotions, is not a religion but a cult. A true religion does not expect you to sacrifice your mind, but it tells you to commit it. If emotionalism turns you "on" and intellectualism turns you "off", then you should take some time to think; Why? Am I immolating the God-given priceless gift of 'Aq'l' (power of reasoning), on an altar, with a sword of devotions and traditions? Am I leading myself with an open mind or being lead by sentimental beliefs? Am I imitating others in a society, so as not to be an outcast?

Sometimes it makes me wonder as to why, a person that would not invest a small portion of his material wealth on the words of his relatives and elders without inquiring and understanding the nature of investment, risk involved and gains expected; would gamble his total spiritual wealth (his soul), on the words of the same relatives and elders without inquiring and understanding the realities and principles of a religion. Furthermore, when confronted with unfavourable or negative feedbacks, he simply shrugs his shoulders, as if the soul he is committing every day is not his. I wish Allah had put a price tag in dollars and cents, on each and every human soul, and collected that sum from the owner, out of his accumulated material wealth. Perhaps then he would not be gambling it so remorselessly.

The realities of the Day of Judgement are not compelling enough to those who have not read the Quran. On that day every individual; not his relatives and elders, will be held responsible for not making use of his 'Aq'l' and giving credence to the unverified claims of his kith and kins, who in turn had done what he is doing today, that is, gambling their souls on the reliances and convictions of their predecessors.

Conviction No. 1:

"Heaven and Hell, (to give) is in my hand."

Many Ismailis do sincerely believe that on the Day of Judgement, Aga Khan will be enthroned upon the Sovereign Throne and he will dispense the Judgement. Their conviction is based upon various Farmans of Aga Khan. Quoted below is one such Farman made in Rajkot, India and published in a book called 'Khangi Farman' (Private Commands), printed in "Khojki"(a secretive script used by Khojas):

"Do not at all ponder about the future and do not at all think over whether you shall receive Heaven or Hell in the hereafter. Because, all things – Heaven and Hell, (to give) is in my hand."

(Dated 20th February, 1910; Page 72)

There are some Ismailis who believe that Aga Khan will not be seated upon the Sovereign Throne, but he will act as their intercessor. Allah will not question them for the sins that Aga Khan or his authorized representatives *(Mukhis and Kamadias)* have forgiven, by giving *'Chhantas'*.

'Chhanta' means sprinkling of (holy) water on the face of an Ismaili when alive or upon his dead body or on the face of his relative after the burial, by Aga Khan's representatives to forgive the sins. An Ismaili takes between 2000 and 5000 *"Chhantas"* during his lifetime and a dozen or so after his death. Of course, there is a fee to be paid for every 'Chhanta'.

Note: It may sound strange and unreal but it is a fact that Aga Khan III, in whose hand was Heaven and Hell and who gave "Chhantas" (forgiving sins) to his followers during his term of Imamat, was given "Chhantas" by one of his own followers *(Mukhi)*, before his burial in Aswan, so that the departed soul may be forgiven! The question is: Forgiven by whom? Mukhi!

Allah says:

> "Give the warning to those in whose (hearts) is the fear that they will be brought (to Judgement) before their Lord, for whom there is no protecting friend **nor intercessor** beside Him (Allah), that they may ward off (evil)" "... and who can forgive sins **except** Allah?"
>
> *Holy Quran 6/51 and 3/135*

There are also Ismailis who believe that Aga Khan will be answerable to Almighty Allah for all his actions, on the Day of Judgement. If it was not so, then why did Ismailis pray for the *'Magpharat'* (Salvation of Soul) of Aga Khan III, for days and weeks, after his death?

Here above, we have perfect examples of irrational convictions overtaking the positive realities. For an outsider to visualize them, with his open mind, is very easy. Whereas, those who have sacrificed their power of reasoning, would be harbouring false vanity, that a devout's reliance on the Farmans of his Imam is beyond human reasoning and logic. Their reliance on Farmans has overshadowed the truth, and the basis of their reliance is emotionalism, which their sentiments and pride would not allow them to admit.

Conviction No. 2:

"Facing Qibla is not a fundamental principal of Islam"

Ismailis do not face in the direction of Mecca, the Islamic Qibla, while reciting their ritual prayers. To uphold and support their Unique Belief, *Al-Waiz* (missionary) Abualy writes:

> "Facing Qibla in prayer is not a fundamental principle of Islam, it is a tradition."
> *'Ismaili Tariqah'* page 184

Is the command of Allah a tradition? Is not obedience to the Command of Allah the most fundamental principle of Islam? What would happen if Ismaili missionaries were to propagate that obedience to the Command of Aga Khan is not a fundamental principle of Ismailism?

Allah Commands:

"From whencesoever thou startest forth (for prayer) turn thy face in the direction of the Sacred Mosque: **That is indeed the truth from thy Lord**. And Allah is not unmindful of what ye do. So from whencesoever thou startest forth, turn thy face in the direction of the Sacred Mosque; among wheresoever ye are turn your face thither: That there be no ground of dispute against you among the people, except those of them that are bent on wickedness; so fear them not, but fear Me; and that I may complete My favours on you, and ye may be guided".

Holy Quran 2/ 149-150

Belief No. 3:

Tawaf of Kabah made obligatory because of Ali!

Below is an extract from 'Ismaili Tariqah', page 208:–

"An eminent Sunni scholar of Nishapur, Maulvi Lutfullah Nishapuri (d. 180 A.H.) wrote:

(A poem in Persian)

Translation by Abualy:

"The circumambulation of the Kaba has been made obligatory for all (Muslims) because this is the birth place of Ali Ibn Abi-Talib."

Ismaili Ginan *"Muman Chetawni"* describes the birth of Ali in Kabah as under which is no less than a fairy tale.

એજી   માતાજી   ગયાતા   બઘતમાંહે,
તાયત   કરવાને   સાર;
ઇબાદત   કરીને   જ્યારે   ઉઠીયાં,
અલી   પેદાની   સમે   થઇ   તેણીજવાર.–ચેતો૦ ૮૦
એજી   તારે   માતાજી   પડીઆં   વીચારમાં,
હવે   ઘેર   ગયાની   નથી   વાર;
તાં   કેક   ઘર   બીજો   હતો,
તેની   ભીંત   ફાટી   બારી   થઇ   તેણીજ   વાર. ચેતો૦ ૮૧
એજી   તારે   માતાજી   ઉઠી   તે   માંહે   ગયા,
હુરાં   બે   આવીયું   તે   ઘર   મીંજર;
તે   સમે   અલી   પેદા   થયા,
તે   બાદ   નીરંજનનું   અવતાર.–ચેતો૦ ૮૨

Translation:

> The mother of Ali had gone to *Baitullah* (Kabah) to pray. When she rose from her worship, it was the time for the birth of Ali. She became worried. There was not time enough to reach home. There was another house nearby. A wall of that house instantly broke open and became a window. She got up and entered. Two *"Hurahs"* (heavenly maids) came into the house. Then Ali was born. He is the *"Avtar"*(incarnation) of the Unseen, from time immemorial.
>
> *"Muman Chetawni", verses 80 to 82*

History records that Ali's father was the son of Abd al-Muttalib ibn Hashim, keeper of the keys of the Kabah (a prestigious post in pre-Islamic society of Mecca). The

Ginan says, she went into another house that was nearby. It could have been the house of the keeper, her father-in-law. Anyone who has read the history of Islam or the Quran knows that Kabah's significance is associated with Abraham and Ishmael and **not** with Ali or his mother.

Where was Karim Aga Khan born?

In 1960, a biography of Karim Aga Khan was published in Gujrati by Aga Khan's institution for the publication of Ismaili literature, the Ismailia Association for India, Bombay. This biography records that **Karim Aga Khan was born in Paris, France.** Ismaili leaders who have been closely associated with the Aga Khans also say he was born in Paris.

In 1970, Willi Frischauer, a hagiographer, published his book *'The Aga Khans'*. The author was given full cooperation by Karim Aga Khan and his office. Willi Frischauer and Al-Waiz Abualy record that **Karim Aga Khan was born in Geneva, Switzerland.**

'Noorum-Mubin' (1951) a book of history of all the Ismaili Imams and Pirs, records that the message of birth came from Geneva, and it was dated 13th of December. 'Noorum-Mubin' does not specify where Karim Aga Khan was born. Author Mihir Bose of *'The Aga Khans'* has avoided the controversy by not mentioning the place of birth. He writes "... less than seven months after the wedding, on 17th December 1936, she (mother of Karim Aga Khan) gave birth to a son."

It is surprising then that Ismaili historians and Ismailis are not positive in which **city** their 49th Imam, Karim Aga Khan, was born in 1936 but they are positive in which **house**, their first Imam, Ali was born 1400 years ago.

When was Prince Aly Khan born?

Abualy writes:

> "He was born on **Tuesday** the thirteenth of June, **1911** at Turin".　　　　(*page 99*)

Noorum-Mubin writes :

> "He was born on **Monday** the 13th June **1910** A.D. i.e. 5th day of Jamadil Akhir in 1328 Hijri, in Turin, Italy."　　(*page 483*)

Conviction No. 4:

"Ithna'asri religion will not exist at all".

Below is a Farman of Aga Khan III, Translated:-

> "...Our religion is based upon '*Aq'l*' (power of reasoning). If you seek religion without 'Aq'l' you will not understand much and will obtain nothing. Within ten, twenty or thirty years, the Ithana'asri religion will be worn-out. After 100 years the Ithna'ashri religion will not exist at all. It will not exist in Iran either because that religion's base is not on Aq'l. Our religion's base is on Aq'l".

A person with 'Aq'l' would realize that the above Farman was made on 13th July 1899 in Zanzibar and today after nearly 90 years the Ithna'ashri religion has been a dominating power in Iran. And, Shias are in absolute majority. On the other hand, in India and Pakistan, more and more Ismailis are openly practicing the true Islam and disassociating themselves from the un-Islamic practices of the Ismaili Tariqah.

Note: The sole object of my quoting this Farman is to prove the point of 'Divine Vision'. I am not an Isthna'ashri.

Conviction No. 5:

"I will send to you the Original Quran".

A Farman of Aga Khan III, translated:

> "Khalifa Usman has removed certain por-
> tions from the Quran-e-Shariff. If I copy
> the Original Quran, it will take six years.
> That too I will send to you, then you will
> notice what has been removed and what
> changes have been done (by Khalifa
> Usman)."

The above Farman was made on 30th July 1899, also in Zanzibar. The Ismailis who have been waiting for the arrival of the Original Quran from their Imam will have to keep waiting, probably to the Day of Judgment. On that day the 'True Realities' will be made known. But, it will be too late to repent.

Conviction No. 6:

... Go to Australia

If Karim Aga Khan were to say; "Move out of Canada, go to Australia", the very next day, Ismailis would start selling their businesses and tender their resignations in a rush to obtain immigration visas for Australia. This is because Ismailis firmly believe their Imam knows precisely what is going to happen the next day, in the next year or in the next century. Their reliance has moulded them to rely and trust the Aga Khan's so-called 'Divine Vision' and the 'Noorani Power'.

My father emigrated from Bombay in the year 1953 and went to East Africa. He wrote a letter to Aga Khan seeking his guidance and blessings for the establishment of his business and a quick settlement in Africa. He was advised to settle himself with his family in the Congo. The rationale given was that the independence of the African countries would commence from British East Africa. **The Congo would be the last to receive its independence.** Similar advice was also given to other Ismailis. My father, being a devout follower of Aga Khan, settled himself in Leopoldville, Belgium Congo (now known as Kinshasha, Zaire), in 1954.

In December 1954, my wife and I had a '*Mulaqat*' (audience) with Aga Khan III and his fourth wife, at Villa Yakimur in Cannes. The Aga Khan asked, if I had made any plans to go to the Congo. I replied; I had not considered it. In March 1955, I received a letter from him in response to my article on the subject of "Ismaili Theory of Ten Incarnations – *Das Avtar*". At the bottom thereof, Aga Khan wrote in his own shaky hand writing:

When do you go to the Congo ? ?

aga khan

My wife and I considered this line of repeated questioning to be an insinuation. In February 1956, I sold my business, disposed of my personal assets, packed my suitcases and moved to Leopoldville with my family. The movement for Independence had already started in Belgium Congo. I left the Congo and came back to Pakistan. In June 1960 Belgium Congo and in August 1960 French Congo became independent. In the entire continent of Africa, **the Congo was the first region to become independent,** as if to prove that no one but Allah alone ever knows what will happen in the future.

Tanganyika became independent in December 1961. Uganda became independent in October 1962. Zanzibar became independent on December 10, 1963. And Kenya, which was supposed to get its independence first, was the last to become independent on December 12, 1963.

Unique Reality

Ismailis would rather obey the Farmans of their Imam than the Commands of Allah – the Quran. This is not only an established practice amongst Ismailis but a fact that has been recorded by the Courts of Law in India, as a piece of evidence. Abualy writes:

> "The Shia Muslims in general, and particularly Ismailis, maintain that no one understands the Holy Quran better than the Holy Prophet and his **Successor Imams**, because it was revealed in **their** House. They, therefore, follow the **interpretation** as taught by their Holy Imams."
>
> 'Ismaili Tariqah' Page 94

Were the verses of the Holy Quran revealed in the house of Ali and his "**Successor Imams**"? Many of the revelations came to the Prophet when he was not in his own house – for example, the very first revelation.

Does the interpretation of the Quran mean authority to (a) abrogate the Commands, (b) to substitute the Commands or (c) to introduce new Commands?

Have not Ismailis (a) abrogated the Command of performing 'Hajj', (b) substituted the Command of fastings during the month of Ramadhan with the fastings of "Beej-Shukarwari" and "Satima no Rozo", and (c) introduced the ceremony of taking "Chhantas" (forgiving sins) at the command of their Imams?

"The Sure Reality"

After having examined the "Unique Reality", let us find out what is "The Sure Reality". Allah (S.W.T.) has revealed an entire 'Sura'(chapter) on **"Haqqa"** (The Sure Reality).

He says:

> "The Sure Reality! What is the Sure Reality? And what will make thee realize what the Sure Reality is?
>
> *Holy Quran 69/1-2-3*

After having asked the questions, Allah (S.W.T.) goes on to explain in detail what happened to the tribes of Thalmud and Aad; rulers such as Pharaoh and those before him, who disregarded the Messages of Allah. How all of them came to a violent end. Their splendor and grandeur, based upon falsehood, were transitory.

Abdullah Yusuf Ali, a well known translator of the Quran, writes in his commentary:

> "Al-haqqa: the sure Truth: the event that must inevitably come to pass; the state in which all falsehood and pretence will vanish, and the absolute Truth will be laid bare".

Allah says:–

> **"In their history verily there is a lesson** for men of understanding.It is no invented story but a confirmation of the existing (Scripture); and a detailed explanation of everything and a guidance and a mercy for folk who believe."
>
> *Holy Quran 12/111*

Allah has recorded in Sura Haqqa (chapter 69) the tragic fate of the people of the pre Quranic era who disregarded His Messages. We will now examine a similar fate of the people of the post revelation era, or to be precise, the violent end of Alamutian Ismailis and their Imams, who had declared freedom from the Quranic Laws. Hopefully, the woeful outcome of events recorded below from the books of history would be a lesson for men of understanding, who believe in the realities of history.

Be my slaves not Allah's

On 17th Ramadan 559 A.H. i.e. 8th August 1164, Imam Hasan, ala Zikrihis Salaam, the 23rd Imam made the following Proclamation:

> "Today......I make you **free from the rigidity of the Law** and resurrect you from the bondage of the letter to the freedom of the spirit of the Law. **Obey me and follow my farma'n ...**"
>
> 'A Brief History of Ismailism', page 73

Note: The Imam made Ismailis free from the bondage of Allah's Law; but, he said: "Obey me and follow my Farma'n". That is : **Be my slaves not Allah's**. After 800 years Ismailis are still slaves of their Imam and would rather obey his Farmans and not those of Allah – the Quranic Laws.

Noorum -Mubin writes:

> By declaring *"Eid-ul-Qiyama"* on the 17th Ramadhan, the 23rd Imam Hasan ala' Zikrihis Salaam had raised the glory of his ancestor Hazrat Ali, who was slain by the

hands of Abdul Rehman ibn Muljim on the same day of 17th Ramadhan and had obtained "freedom from the world" and had made "Union with God".

Ismailis believe that since they have made a Union with the 'Noor of Allah' *(Imam-e Zaman)* they too have obtained the freedom from the Quranic Laws and entered the realm of Noor.

History records:

> One and half years after the Proclamation of *"Eid-ul Qiyama"*(the Unique Realities), the 23rd Imam, the proclaimer of the Proclamation and leader of the Assassins was **assassinated** with a dagger (traditional weapon of the Assassins), by his own brother-in-law on 10th January, 1166. The 24th and 25th Imams died of **poisoning** in 1210 and 1221. The next Imam, the 26th, was **murdered** in 1255 and the last Imam of the Alamut, the 27th Imam was captured and drowned in a river by the army of Halaku Khan, the grandson of Ghenghis Khan.

In **less than a century** from the proclamation of the Freedom from Law, the empire of Ismailis (Assassins) **met it's violent fate and came to an end.** All the forts of Alamut, Lamasar, Rudbar, Kohistan and others were completely destroyed. Most of these forts were destroyed and levelled by Ismailis themselves at the command of their last Imam, Rukn al-Din Khurshah. He was following the orders of Halaku Khan, for the destruction of these forts, one after another, in return for the safety of his own life and that of his family members. Finally he surrendered to the Mongolian army; hoping he and his family and his last fort would be spared, but they drowned him in a river, killed each and every Ismaili and destroyed the last fort of the Assassins.

Professor Bernard Lewis writes:

"On the edge of the Khangay range, on the way back to Persia, he (Rukn al-Din) was led away from the road, on the pretext of going to a feast, and was murdered ... The destruction of Alamut, and the final humbling of Ismaili power, are vividly depicted by (Ata Malik) Juvayni. 'In that breeding-ground of heresy in the Rudbar of Alamut the home of the wicked adherents of Hasan-i Sabbah ... there remains not one stone of the foundations upon another. And in that flourishing abode of innovation the Artist of Eternity Past wrote with the pen of violence upon the portico of each one's dwelling the verse: "These their empty houses are empty ruins." *(Quran, xxvii, 53)* And in the market-place of those wretches' kingdom the muezzin Destiny has uttered the cry of "Away then with the wicked people!" *(Quran, xxiii, 43)* Their luckless womenfolk, like their empty religion, have been utterly destroyed. And the gold of those crazy, double-dealing counterfeiters which appeared to be unalloyed, has proven to be base lead."

'The Assassins – A Radical Sect of Islam'
page 95

Noorum-Mubin (1951), records on page 303:

"The pages after pages of history books are filled with details of Halaku Khan's huge mass killings, plunders, inhuman cruel burnings and atrocities. He did not spare the six month old children who were in their cradles". "Imam was drowned in a river."

This is not an invented story but a record from history confirming the scripture and **"Haqqa"** (the Sure Realities). When history is repeated, the falsehood and pretence will once more perish and the Word of Allah will prevail.

Allah says:

"We have sent them the Truth; but they indeed practise Falsehood!"
'Holy Quran' 23/90

"When it is said to them: 'Come to what Allah hath revealed, and to the Apostle': Thou seest the Hypocrites avert their faces from thee in disgust". "Those men, – Allah knows what is in their hearts; so keep clear of them, **but admonish them, and speak to them a word to reach their very souls"**.
'Holy Quran' 4/61 & 63

Note: It is a sacred duty of every Muslim to preach and warn his fellow Muslims, perchance they may fear Him. For more information read Holy Quran 7/163-164.

13

Unique Confession

Judaism, Christianity and Islam

A great historian of religion devoted forty years of his life to determining what the world's religions have in common, and came up with two things: "Belief in God — if there be a God," and "Life is worth living — sometimes."

That was the point of view of a historian — one who narrates past events. If a theologian — one who analyses the scriptures, was to devote that many years of his life to determine what the major religions of the world have in common, then he would come up with one thing: "A thread is woven through the cardinal principles of Judaism, Christianity, and Islam. The Prophets of these three great religions have taught one lesson over and over again – the **monotheism**". The spiritual development of mankind has been gradual and in stages, like the physical development of a child. Lord the Almighty, has been sending His Messengers to warn mankind about attributing His Glory to others and associating partners to him. He is Absolute. Each Prophet brought the concept of ONE GOD, as Cardinal Principle of God's religion, and submission to that ONE GOD ALONE as the fundamental credo and profession of faith.

Prophet Musa (s.a.s.), (*in Latin* – Moses) formed a centre of consolidation for the early Semitic tribes. From there on, their acceptance of Yahweh as God, rather than their tribal ancestry, made them Jews. God gave to the children of Israel the great credo, '*Shema*':

"Hear, O Israel; The Lord our God is ONE LORD."

Deut. 6/4

The Israelites were then practicing Baalism, serving graven images, worshipping heavenly hosts, and venerating the Sun god, which they had learnt from the Egyptians, Babylonians, and Canaanite tribes.

History of the Prophets of the Middle East records that with the exception of Islam, every time a Prophet had departed from amongst his people, the followers had, in one way or another, reverted to the practice of associating others with the Absolute Being. Whilst Moses was on the mountain receiving God's Commandments, the Israelites became impatient, and led by Samiri, formed a molten statue of a golden calf or a gold plated wooden calf. They worshipped it, sacrificed to it, bowed before it, ate, drank, and revelled in song and dance surrounding the calf which represented God.

The Jews had not fully understood and accepted the Command of worshipping **"One Lord"** of great 'Shema', although 'Shema' was on their lips, in their prayers, and placed on the posts of their front doors. History confirms the fact that Judaism until as late as the advent of Islam had pictures of Sun gods and heavenly hosts in the Synagogues. The large central medallion of the mosaic floor in Bet Alpha Synagogue (6th Century A.D.) had Helios driving the horses of the Sun God surrounded by the signs of the Zodiac. The four seasons were pictured in the four corners of the medallion. After seeing the Islamic Mosques decorated with floral and geometric patterns and the artistic calligraphy that not only adorned the House of God, but also conveyed His message, the Jews began changing the pattern of decorating their Synagogues.

The mission of Moses for establishing "Unity of God" was not completed. The Bible records that seven centuries before the coming of Jesus Christ, King Josiah (622 B.C.) burnt down the wooden chariots of the Sun god and vessels made for Baal (the god of fertility), which were kept in the house of the Lord by the Jewish high priests.

Besides, the Jewish community had monopolized on the words **"our** God" of their capsule credo – the 'Shema', and made their religion and God, sectarian and prepossessed. They had built high walls surrounding the religion, taught by Prophet Moses. The Message of God became non-universal and exclusive for the tribes of Israel. The name Yisra'el is explained through popular etymology as "He contends against El (God)".

The Almighty now sent another Messenger of His, named Issa (s.a.s.), (*in Latin* – Jesus). Being anointed he became Jesus Christ. It is recorded that, when a man versed in "the Law" (*the Old Testament*) asked Jesus

Christ, "Teacher, which is the greatest Commandment in the Bible?" Jesus quoted the First Commandment, **"Thou shalt have no other gods before Me"** and added, "You must Love the Creator your God with your whole heart and with your whole soul and with your whole mind."

The Message that Jesus had brought was the same as declared in the fifth Book of Moses, called Deuteronomy, which is:

"Thou shalt have no other gods before Me."

"Thou shalt not bow down thyself unto them, nor serve them; for I the Lord thy God am a jealous God..."

In other words, God not only resents the idea of associating a partner or partners to Him, but takes most serious offence at the concept of sharing His Glory, because He is the SOLE OWNER of that Glory. The lesson that Jesus had taught was of believing, obeying, serving, praying to and loving ONE GOD, whom he used to call my Father and your Father in the Heaven. The philosophical and spiritual statements of Jesus were misinterpreted by the Apostles after his departure. The misunderstood relationship of "my Father" made him the only "begotten" son of the Heavenly Father, in its physical sense and meaning. Centuries later Trinitarian terms were added by the Church, to the Biblical description of "ONE GOD". The term Trinity is not a divine revelation; neither the word 'Trinity', nor the explicit doctrine of Trinity, appear in the Bible. It developed several centuries after the departure of Jesus and through many controversies.

In John 1:14, the Divine Command, "The Word" became "The God", when *theos* (God) at the end of the verse, John 1:1 became *"ho theos"* (the God) in its interpretation of John 1:14. In other words, "Theos", that described the nature of "the Word" (which was Divine) was identified with his person as "the God." Actually, in the Greek text, the definite article *"ho"*, (the), appears before the first "God", but there is no article before the second. Moreover, the phrase "with God" in the middle of the verse, John 1:1, separates the entity of God from "the Word".

On the same subject of Divine Command, Quran teaches that when Allah commands "BE; 'it happens'. It was a Divine Command (the Word "BE") that brought forth Flesh or "The Command" was made flesh. In the words of John 1:14, "The Word was made flesh", in the womb of the Virgin Mary. The Quran acknowledges the birth of Jesus from his mother Mary, who was a virgin. To ward off skepticism, it goes further and explains that, if God could create Adam without a Father and Mother, then it is not difficult for Him to create someone with Mother alone by His Command..

It is interesting to note that to reinforce the theory of **"the only begotten Son"**, in John 1:14 – the verse on the basis of which the said concept is advocated – after the words *"And the Word was made flesh, and dwelt among us"*, the following phrases have been **added, within brackets**, in the middle of the verse:

> "**...** (and we beheld his glory, the glory as of the only begotten of the Father)..."
> *Authorized King James Version, John 1:14*

As for Christ, the resurrected **Saviour**, the Bible says:

> "I, even I, am the Lord; and beside me there is **no saviour**."
> *Isaiah 43:11*

– 154 –

"... and there is no God else beside me; a just God and **a Saviour**; there is none beside me."

Isaiah 45:21

Christianity lost the monotheism to theomorphism when it made its great founder, Jesus Christ, not only the chosen Prophet and Messenger of God, but also a God incarnated or embodied, having been begotten in a physical form. The 'Unity of God' – the Absolute Being – was forsaken. It adopted the idea of *"Unity in Trinity"*. It is a belief in Him, that exists in three parts, yet remaining one God. The first part is God Himself as Father, the second part is God the Son that is Begotten, and the third part is God the Holy Spirit that emanates. Islam says: God does not emanate from anything. He is Absolute Original. God is not begotten. He does not beget. Anything that is begotten matures and becomes like its parents. The son becomes the father and the daughter becomes the mother. Thus, there would be two Gods and when the begotten one begets, there would be more than two Gods. The Church of Jesus had forgotten the original Command: **"Thou shalt have no other gods before Me"**, which equally applied to "God the Son" and to "God the Holy Spirit".

God now sent Muhammad (s.a.s.) and gave the concept of *"Allah"*. Allah is formed by joining the definite article *"Al"* (meaning "The") with *"Illah"* (God). Literally, Allah means 'The God', not 'God' or 'A God', for there is only ONE GOD. Allah is the Almighty Creator and Sustainer of all upon this world as well as of all upon all the other worlds. He is therefore called *"Rabbil alamin"* – the Cherisher and Sustainer of the worlds. He is not just for a particular group or race of people. His Message (the Quran) is for mankind in its entirety and not only for Muslims. **His Message is universal and eternal**.

The Quran confirms the previous scriptures because the Prophets that brought them were all sent by One God. It repeats some of the stories of the previous scriptures because the originator and inspirer is the same One God. The Quranic text has been free from human editing and consequently stories are neither exaggerated nor understated, hence more logical and coherent.

God gave through Muhammad "*Shahadah*", instead of "*Shema*". The root word of Shema is "to hear", whereas the root word of "Shahadah" is "to confess". Mankind had been hearing about "ONE GOD" for a long time. Now the time had come to "confess" aloud, from the heart, what it had been hearing. The spiritual development of the human race has been like that of a child who had been hearing names and relating them to persons and things and then begins repeating the same words and names with the knowledge and understanding of their meanings and relationships. God says:

> "Say: He is Allah, The One and Only; Allah, the Eternal, Absolute; He begot no one, nor was He begotten. And there is none like unto Him."
>
> *Holy Quran 112 / 1 to 4*

No person can claim to be a Muslim unless he or she recites and bears witness with heartfelt conviction: "*There is no God but Allah, and Muhammad is His Prophet*". Anyone who negates the above "confession of faith" (Shahadah) is a non-Muslim.

Anyone who associates other god or gods besides God has not surrendered himself fully to One God. This has been the eternal Message that God has been repeating again and again through various Messengers. The Islam acknowledges these Messengers that came before Muhammad and there are recitals of Aaron, Abraham, Adam,

David, Elias, Elijah, Ishmael, Issac, Jacob, Jesus, Job, John the Baptist, Jonah, Joseph, Lot, Mary, Moses, Noah, Saul, Soloman, Zechariah and others in the Quran.

Abdul-Khaliq, but not Khaliq

Abdul-Khaliq was an office-bearer of the Ismailia Council in Kuwait and a friend of mine. Often, he would come to Karachi to see his relatives. We used to call him Khaliq (a short for Abdul-Khaliq), whenever he was in Karachi. One day I was in Kuwait and wanted to speak to Abdul-Khaliq. I picked up a telephone, dialed his office number and asked his secretary: "Can I please speak to **Khaliq**?".

My friend's secretary was a Muslim lady from Kuwait. She answered back: "La" meaning "No", or that is to say, "There is no Khaliq" and she hung up. I tried again, asked the same question and she gave me the same reply and hung up. That day I must have tried several times, each time hoping that my friend must have now returned to his office. But everytime the lady would shout louder and hang up. In the evening I met Abdul-Khaliq in the Kuwait Jamatkhana (most of the Jamatkhanas in Middle East and Malaysia are now closed permanently). I asked my friend if he was in his office that day. He replied; yes. Thereupon I mentioned what had happened over the phone. He immediately understood the problem, because, I was not the first Pakistani friend of his to have encountered it.

Abdul-Khaliq then gave me an explanation for his secretary's action and that was my lesson in *"Tawheed"* (Unity of Allah). He mentioned that if his secretary had passed the call to him, then it would be a confirmation on her part, that she has recognized my friend as "Khaliq"; which literally translated "a Creator". Such a confirmation would constitute "*Shirk*", meaning she had associated someone else beside Allah as a Creator. In Islam, "Shirk" is an unpardonable sin because it repudiates "Tawheed" (Unity or Oneness of Allah) and disowns the "Shahadah" (the confession of faith). My friend suggested that in future I should ask for him by his full name, Abdul-Khaliq (slave of the Creator), and not as Khaliq. Remember: **There is no Khaliq but the Khaliq**.

Two Confessions

The Ismaili Tariqah being a Unique Tariqah, has two Shahadahs, like two sets of teeth of an elephant. A Shahadah that is visible like a protruding tusk is published in the book of Ismaili Constitution. The second Shahadah that is hidden like a set of chewing teeth is published in the book of Ismaili Dua. The '*Shahadah*' (Confession of Faith) of the Constitution is the same as recorded above. It is one that any Muslim would recite and confess. The '*Shahadah*' of the *Dua* (ritual prayer) has an extra phrase annexed to it. This annexed phrase **negates the "Unity of God'** by confessing: "The Ali, the God."

Below are the photographic reproductions of the Ismaili 'Kalimah Shahadah' with its transliteration and translations from the book of Ismaili Dua, published by The Shia Imami Ismailia Association for Africa, Kenya, 1963.

لَا إِلَهَ إِلَّا اللهُ مُحَمَّدُ الرَّسُولُ اللهِ - عَلِىٌّ

أَمِيرُ الْمُؤْمِنِينَ عَلِىُّ اللهِ -

La ilaha illallaha, Mohammedur-Rasoolullahi,
Aliyyun   Amirul-mu'mineen   Aliyyullah:

There is no deity except Allah, Muhammad is the Messenger of Allah, Aly, the master of the believers, is from Allah,

અલ્લાહ સિવાય બીજા કોઇ મઅબુદ (ઇબાદતને લાયક) નથી. મુહમ્મદ અલ્લાહના પયગમ્બર છે. અલી, સાચા દીનદારોના સરદાર, અલ્લાહમાંથી છે (અને તે એજ છે)

The phrase that negates the *"Tawheed"* (Unity of Allah) is *"Aliyyullah"* عَلِيُّ اللّٰه It appears at the end of the Shahadah. This phrase is a combination of two words.

"Aliyyun" عَلِيٌّ and *"Allah"* اللّٰه When the two are joined together, they read "Aliyyullah". The word *"Aliyyun"* means "The Ali" and *"Allah"* means "The God". Hence, the phrase "Aliyyullah" means "The Ali, the God", which also signifies "The Aga Khan, The God".

As an example, if I was to write "The Abualy, The Missionary", it would mean "That particular Abualy (*is*) the Missionary". To contend and say that I have meant "That particular Abualy is *from* the missionary" is totally incorrect and unfactual. Hence, the English translation, which reads "Aly...is *from* Allah" is a baseless smoke screen. The Arabic word for "from" is *"min"*, and it does not appear in the Arabic text. Therefore, it is not incorrect to say that the Ismaili Kalimah Shahadah negates the "Unity of Allah".

I remember the answer given by Abualy. An Ismaili questioned: What is the difference between the Kalimah of our old Dua, wherein we used to recite 'Ali sahi (truly)

Allah', and of the new Dua which recites "Aliyyullah"? Abualy's response was: There is no difference. He added, while demonstrating: We (Ismailis) used to hold our ear with our hand from the front – across the chest. Now we are holding the same ear with the same hand but from the back of our neck. In other words; Aga Khan is truly Allah.Ismailis are not raising their voices for the removal of the last phrase of their Kalimah. But they all know that one day, even if not today, they could be thrown out of the fold of Islamic *Ummah* (Brotherhood), especially in Pakistan, for their un-Islamic Kalimah. Equating Aga Khan with Allah is far worse than the equating of Mirza Gulam Ahmed with Prophet Muhammad by Qaddiyanis *(Ahmediyyas)*, who have recently been declared "non-Muslims" by the Law in Pakistan.

Today, many Ismailis in India and Pakistan have given up the recitation of the Ismaili Dua. More Ismailis are openly reciting Islamic *Namaz* (Salat). Ismailia Namazi Khidmat Committee of Pakistan has constructed two *Masjids* (Mosques) in Karachi to recite Azan and Namaz with other Ismailis in congregation. Similarly, in India, Islah Educational Foundation of Bandra, Bombay has constructed a Mosque for Ismailis of Bombay and is now constructing a 13.18 million rupees complex in the town of Tighra in the District of Valsad. The project includes Boarding House, Sanatorium, Medical Centre, Buildings for Secondary, Technical, and also Social Education where the Boarders will learn to recite the entire Quran by heart, call the Azan and lead the Namaz.

I have been informed from several sources that a draft of 'Namaz for Ismailis' has been submitted by the Institute of Ismaili Studies, London, to the office of Karim Aga Khan in France for signature and promulgation. The need for change has been perceived as more acute sinceJune 1986 when a group of Ismailis filed a civil suit in the High Courts of Sind at Karachi, Pakistan, for the right of Ismailis to recite Azan and Namaz in Jamatkhanas. The judgment is expected very soon. Whatever the eventual outcome, however, this litigation has raised some eye-brow raising questions in the minds of local Muslims, through the Pakistani media. The case has generated momentum from the non-Ismaili Muslims, many of whom have come out in the open supporting the plaintiffs. It will not be an easy task for the Courts of an Islamic Republic to restrict Ismaili Muslims from reciting Namaz in a House of Prayer built for Ismaili Muslims.

However, the Defendants are trying their best to sway the decision in their favour, by making a submission in their Counter-Affidavit, that "Inherent right of devolution of ownership of Jamatkhanas (is) in the Imam"; "Jamatkhanas are not dedicated as Masjids" and historically, such establishments are "additional places for religious practices, other than Masjids, for supererogatory prayers".

Note: The above mentioned sworn statement acknowledges that a Jamatkhana is a place for supererogatory prayer but not a place for *Sujood* (Prostration) – the root word for Masjid. Do not Ismailis make *Sujoods* in their *Dua?* Literally, Masjid means, a place for making Sujood.

"O Ali – You the Creator – You the Judge"

I have met hundreds of educated Ismailis who take pride in declaring themselves as unorthodox Ismailis. They say they are not like other traditional, ill-advised Ismailis who call *Hazar Imam* (Aga Khan) God. They only consider him their religious leader and head of the community. The most surprising thing is that most of these Ismailis who call themselves unorthodox and do not believe in the Divinity of the Aga Khans, send their children to the religious night schools in Jamatkhanas.

One of the most popular and elementary Ginans that these youngsters are taught in the religious night schools is "*Haqq tu – Pak tu*". It is one of the most frequently recited Ginan in the Jamatkhanas.

What does the Ginan "*Haqq tu – Pak tu*" pronounce and declare? It says, O Ali (meaning the Aga Khan) you alone are:

Haqq tu = You the Truth

Pak tu = You the Holy

Sarjanhar tu = You the Creator

Rabb tu = You the Sustainer

Rehman tu = You the Mercy

Kazi tu = You the Judge

Badshah tu = You the King

Awwal tu = You the Beginning

Akhir tu = You the Ending

Zahir tu = You the Seen One

Batin tu = You the Unseen

Ya Ali tuhi tu = O Ali, you alone are you.

I do not see any difference whatsoever between Ismailis who boast that they do not call Aga Khan God, and then teach their children "Haqq tu – Pak tu" and a father who would boast that he is a teetotaller (anti-alcoholic) and then sends his son or daughter to a pub to learn how to drink alcohol.

Note: There is every possibility that the author of the Ginan might have written, in the last verse "*Ya Al-*

lah tuhi tu" = "O Allah, you alone are You", which could have been changed to *"Ya Ali tuhi tu"* by Ismailis.

Allah says:

> "And if it be said unto them: Follow that which Allah hath revealed, they say: Nay, but we follow that wherein we found our fathers. What! Even though the devil were inviting them unto the doom of (blazing) fire?"
>
> *Holy Quran 31/21*

> "And Satan will say when the matter is decided: 'It was Allah who gave you a promise of Truth; I too promised, but I failed in my promise to you. I have no authority over you except to call you, but you obeyed me; **so blame me not, but blame yourselves.** I cannot help you, nor can you help me. Lo! I had already beforehand rebelled against God with whom you associated me. Lo! For wrong-doers there must be a grievous penalty".
>
> *Holy Quran 14/22*

14

Path to Peace

"O Believers, enter into Peace, all together."
Holy Quran

"What is next?"

One Sunday morning, I was awakened from my peaceful sleep by the telephone. It was around seven o'clock. I picked it up. On the other end was an Ismaili missionary calling long distance. He is a well educated, outspoken, middle-aged preacher with western concepts and innovative ideas – a rare combination for an Ismaili missionary.

He had come across some of my papers and questionnaires on the subjects of Ismaili Tariqah, probably passed on to him by members of his congregations. His primary interest was to know if I had received any response to my questionnaires on the Ismaili Traditions and Dua, from any of his fellow missionaries or the institutions that look after the propagation of Ismaili faith. I explained to him that I had mailed the papers to The Institute of Ismaili Studies, London and to The Ismailia Associations all across the world but unfortunately none of them had answered or came forth to have either private or public dialogues on the issues. Probably the matter for discussion was too hot. He remarked; the matter is uncomfortably warm and there are only a few trained firefighters (missionaries), the rest are only dressed like firefighters. He requested me to mail him a few more papers and details on subject matters where ambiguities were prevalent.

A few weeks later, on a Sunday morning when it is cheaper to call from the States, we were again discussing the issues over the telephone. He concluded by asking me a question. He said, "the arguments that you have put forth are of a fundamental nature. The questions you want to be answered are key issues. Your line of interrogation is logical. Even if we were to go to the extent of admitting that your concerns are well founded, what is your suggestion? What do you want us to do? Do we do this ... or this ... or that? My question to you is — **what is next?**"

This same question is being asked over and over again by Ismailis, especially in the 80's. The recent publication of *'The Aga Khans'* by Mihir Bose, articles by foreign journalists in international magazines on the life of the Aga Khans and his followers, letters to editors, open questionnaires and public appeals to Aga Khan through the media have made the Ismailis, intellectually curious and eager for knowledge. Contradictory records from Ismaili history have added fuel to some of the age old burning questions. Today, Ismailis are discussing issues and topics in the open, about which they would not be candid two or three decades ago. When ambiguities and uncertainties continue to prevail, the question is – **what is next**? Before I answer the question, let me briefly elaborate the goal.

"Dar-us-Salaam"

Come winter and every year the migrating birds begin their journey to the South from Alaska and North Canada – most of them reach their destinations. But on their path, a few of them get stranded or waylaid.

I often wonder, were my forefathers lured or got stranded, in their journey to *'Dar-us-Salaam'* (House of Peace)? I am told their aim was freedom from idol worshipping; a journey from theomorphism to monotheism. A pilgrimage from Hinduism to Islam. The question is, "did they or their descendants – my parents – reach their destination?" I am positive my parents and grandparents worshipped Aga Khan as "Sahi (truly) Allah", because they taught me to worship him, the way they did. Hence, I think they, along with hundreds of thousands of their brothers and sisters, were waylaid or lost on their migratory trip to Islam – a true monotheism.

The journey for my parents and grandparents came to an end, when their souls departed from this world. For their brothers and sisters who are alive, the journey is not yet over. The Path to Peace is open for those who wish to continue the march. A peace, that is within and without; no *'taqiyya'* (concealment of faith), no double standards, no 'Unity' in Duality or Trinity. A monotheism that is pure and simple, open and honest. A relationship that is unmediated; no intervening agent(s), no human bondage, no shackles of Constitutions or Clergy. A Peace that has the harmony of body, mind and soul. The goal is to reach that *Dar-us-Salaam* (House of Peace).

Our existence for it is short. So take heart, ponder for whatever time is left with you out of the unknown and act. *Insha-Allah, Fadhlun min Rabbi, fathun qareeb.*

The Journey

Every journey begins with the first step.

"... Lo! Allah changeth not the condition of a folk until they (first) change that which is in their hearts ..."
Holy Quran 13/11

Step No. 1:

A drowning person can only be pulled aboard a ship by a Captain if he is holding a rope coming from that ship. If he holds two ropes coming from two ships, he faces the danger of being torn apart rather than being rescued. Evaluate, do you fear the primary authority or the secondary authorities? Who should you trust, the Creator Himself or His creations? After having evaluated, make a **firm decision** to obey and pray to that **alone** whom you have chosen as your Captain and Rescuer.

"Allah has said: 'Take not (for worship) two gods: For He is just One Allah; then fear Me (and Me alone)'."
Holy Quran 16/51

Step No. 2:

No teacher can write a fresh lesson on a slate that is already filled with old lessons. **Clean your slate without any hesitation**. If the old lesson that you had learnt was 'The Truth', then Allah will not mislead you to other than 'The Truth'. Not cleaning the slate proves that you have not sincerely embarked upon a project of knowing the Truth but your object is to collect facts and evidences that would support and strengthen a particular truth, that you happen to possess by inheritance or acquaintance. In other words you have not chosen Him as your Teacher with complete confidence.

> "When My servants ask thee concerning Me, I am indeed close (to them); I listen to the prayer of every suppliant when he calleth on Me: Let them also, **with a will**, listen to My Call, and **believe in Me**; that they may walk in the right way."
>
> *Holy Quran 2/186*

Step No. 3:

We have cleaned our slates. Now where is the lesson? Allah says:

> "And We have revealed the Book to thee for the express purpose, that thou mayst explain unto them that wherein they differ, and that it should be **a guide** and a mercy to those who believe."
>
> *Holy Quran 16/64*

Step No. 4:

Having accepted that the Revelations of Allah – the Quran – as our teacher, we consider which version of the

– 168 –

Quran to read. First of all, the concept of the existence of more than one version of the Quran is incorrect. In the case of the Holy Bible, there are several versions, e.g., Vulgate, Wycliff, Tyndale, the Authorised Version (King James Version), the Revised Standard Versions and so forth. Even the Revised Version of 1952 is re-revised in 1971. There are textual differences and contrasts between these versions. Whereas, since the last 1400 years, the Arabic text of the Quran has not been revised or altered. The differences that we see lie in its translations, interpretations and commentaries. So, the question would be, which is the correct interpretation? How do we know it is not biased or misleading? Allah, *subhanhu wa ta'ala*, has already solved this problem. He says:

> "He it is who hath revealed unto thee (Muhammad) the Scripture wherein are **clear revelations** – they are the substance of the Book – and others (are) allegorical. But those in whose hearts is doubt pursue, forsooth, that which is allegorical seeking (to cause) dissension by seeking to explain it. None knoweth its explanation save Allah. And those who are of sound instruction say: We believe therein; the whole is from our Lord; but only men of understanding really heed."
>
> *Holy Quran 3/7*

This verse makes it clear that the verses of the Quran that are clear to understand, meaning verses of explicit instructions, are the substance or nucleus of the Quran. They are the basic messages and fundamental commands.

Step No. 5:

How do we understand the rest of the Message? Once we have read the clear and explicit Message of the Quran, and continue observing the rules of practical conduct and the prescribed statutes, then He with His Mercy will guide us unto the finer things. Allah, had He willed, would have made us all into one community and expanded equal understandings, but He wants to test us with what He has prescribed. Our duty is to follow His plan, obey the Law prescribed, do good deeds, and strive as in a race for His Mercy. He will then gradually show us the traced out way for the finer things. He will keep opening up the 'Open Way.' "How?" This entire process has been beautifully explained in the Quran. The prescribed Statute is called *"Shirat"* and the prescribed or traced out way or 'Open Way' is called *"Minhaaja"* by Allah in the Quran. For full details please open chapter 5 and read verse 48 in Pickthall's or 51 in Yusuf Ali's translations. I have not quoted the verse this time for the simple reason that I would like you to read the preceding verses, which are also relevant to the subject. The more you read the Quran, the more you will know the answer to "What next?" and "How?"

Step No. 6:

You can call this a word of caution: please **DO NOT** break the covenant that you make with your Creator. Please make it a commitment that when you say "Thee Alone we worship, and Thee Alone we ask for help" (*Iyyaaka na'budu, wa iyyaaka nastaiin*) you mean to abide by it. The moment you call upon "other than Allah" for **Madad** (help) or **Muskil Ashan** (Succor), you have nullified "Thee Alone", the heart and soul of the covenant. And you have scized the second rope.

"Lo! As for those who believe not in the here-after, We have made their deeds fair-seeming unto them; and so they wander about in distraction."

Holy Quran 27/4

"Unto Him is the real prayer. Those unto whom they pray beside Allah respond to them not at all, save as (is the response to) one who stretcheth forth his hands towards water (asking) that it may come unto his mouth, and it will never reach it. **The prayer of disbelievers goeth astray.**"

Holy Quran 13/14

Peace of Allah be upon you.

Should I be a Silent Spectator?

There was a community of fishermen living in a seaside town. These fishermen were Jews and were commanded to observe the Sabbath (Jewish day of worship and rest), decreed upon them by Mosaic Law (The Pentateuch). Many persisted in breaking the Sabbath by fishing between Friday sunset to Saturday sunset, instead of resting and praying.

Allah says in the Quran:

> *"... For on the day of their Sabbath their fish did come to them, openly holding up their heads, but on the day they had no Sabbath, they came not: Thus did We make a trial of them, for they were given to transgression."*

The traditional story relates that some of these fishermen were smart. Instead of defying the Law in the open, they constructed huge reservoirs channelled into the sea. They would allow the fish to swim into the reservoirs on the Sabbath day and in the evening they would trap the fish in the reservoirs by shutting the gates of the channels. The next day they would do the fishing from the reservoirs. This kind of circumvention, as well as the open transgression, divided the community into three groups.

Group A. *Repeatedly transgressed the Sabbath.*
Group B. *Observed the Sabbath.*
Group C. *Observed the Sabbath and preached to group A.*

Thereupon some of the Jews said to the people who were preaching:

> "... Why do ye preach to a people whom Allah will destroy or visit with a terrible punishment? ..."

Allah says, the preachers replied:

> **"... To discharge our duty to your Lord, and perchance they may fear Him."**

Commenting on the above verses (7 / 163-164), translator Abdullah Yusuf Ali writes:

> "There are always people who wonder, no doubt sincerely, what good it is to preach to the wicked. The answer is given to them here: (1) every man who sees evil must speak out against it; it is his duty and responsibility to God; (2) there is always a chance that the warning may have effect and save a precious soul."

After having read the book, if you believe it is your duty and responsibility to Allah, to warn your fellow brothers and sisters, please do not be a silent spectator. **Spread the Truth**. Perchance you may save a soul or two.

'Jazakum Allahu Khairan'.

☐   YES, I'd like to spread the Truth.
       Send me information on Special Propagation Discounts
       for *'Understanding Ismailism'*.

Name _____

Address _____

Postal/Zip Code _____

Phone _____

Mail to: **A.M. TRUST**
          P.O. Box 82584
          BURNABY, B.C.
          Canada V5C 5Z1

REVIEW –

"A colorful and energetic polemic against Ismailism by a former Ismaili – and therefore replete with secrets, anecdotes, indiscretions.

The author now takes his stand as a Muslim. In his treatment of historical Ismailism as falsification one may also trace its history as the institutionalization of an event that was meant to remain purely esoteric – the history of Ismailism as a **betrayal** of its essential ahistoricity.

". . . A lively and readable work of great value to all specialists whatever their own stands may be."

Peter Lamborn Wilson
Author of 'Scandal'
Essays in Islamic Heresy